Copyright © 2024 by Mark E. Kauffman
All rights reserved. This book or any portion thereof
may not be reproduced or used in any manner whatsoever
without the express written permission of the publisher
except for the use of brief quotations in a book review.

Printed in the United States of America

First Printing, 2024

INK Publishing Company, LLC
120 E. Washington St.
New Castle, PA 16101

www. drmarkkauffman.org/ink-publishing/

THE ETHOS INITIATIVE:

RELEASING THE DESTINY OF CITIES

Acknowledgments

I would like to acknowledge and thank our network members of the International Network of Kingdom Leaders for allowing me to develop, teach, practice, and examine the principles that the Holy Spirit has given me within this book.

To my beloved wife Jill, my bride of 35 years, thank you for your support, love, encouragement, and guidance over the years as we have learned together how to RELEASE THE DESTINY of our city New Castle, Pennsylvania. I love you with my life!

To Theresa Burnworth, one of our editors at INK publishing, thank you for your excellent work editing this book, your work is phenomenal.

Finally, to my teacher, the Holy Ghost, who continually reveals His truths from His Holy Word. Thank you for entrusting me to write "THE ETHOS INITIATIVE."

Foreword by Bishop Lonnie Langston

There are myriads in the Body of Christ today that have no real direction in life. They have yet to discover their assignment and purpose, therefore their lives are never complete. The Mega church movement today focuses on "How to fill the house," " More and Better Entertainment," and "How to keep the crowd coming," etc. There's nothing wrong with these programs, but the questions are, "Are we affecting the city by changing lives?" and "Are we impacting untouched parts of the city we are in?" God told Jermiah, "Seek the peace of the city where you are" (Jermiah 29:7). Messiah Jesus' last words before He was taken up into Heaven in Acts 1 were: "Teach All Nations What I Have Taught You." We're not only to teach, but to "train and equip the nation wherein we dwell and the nations."

I have been in full time ministry for 57 years. I've had the privilege of ministering in 70 nations, building churches, Bible institutes, medical clinics, and ordaining untold numbers of men and women. As I look back, I regret that there was not a book available like Apostle Kauffman has written with *The Ethnos Initiative: Releasing the Destinies of Cities* for the Apostolic and Prophetic Ministries that I encountered.

Dr. Kauffman left no stone unturned as he scribed words directly from the throne room. Holy Spirit poured out of him the many, many years of experience in training other pastors and leaders to go deeper into the Kingdom Revelation and make it simple enough to understand while profound enough to provoke even those whom we consider the be cutting edge ministries.

Communities, states, countries, marketplace corporations, business schools and the like will be impacted and elevated beyond where they've walked before.

The glorious understanding and revelation that Apostle Kauffman walks in is beyond that of so many leaders today. There's a phrase often used in motivational circles that says, " Revelation Without Manifestation Brings Frustration." These writings will open revelation of True Kingdom Principles causing manifestation to flow like a river through the sincere and hungry believers.
As this book is digested, I do believe Apostles, Prophets, Evangelists, Pastors, and Teachers will do what they've never done before because they will become whom they've never been before because now they will be whom God always intended them to be therefore fulfilling their assignment in life.

WELL DONE, Beloved Apostle.

Introduction

It's our SET TIME! It's time the demonic canopy is eliminated from our cities and the canopy of God's Kingdom and Glory moves over our cities! Seeds have been sown; now harvest is imminent. This is a critical time in the history of the church and our cities!

We must arise and take our seat of authority and RULE over principalities and powers as royal kings! We must cleanse the Heavens and change geographical climates in which demonic influences have ruled so that a mighty harvest of souls and wealth can be captured and restored into Christ's Kingdom! We must appropriate our royal authority and dethrone the powers of darkness.

The hour has come to reform the landscape of our territory and colonize the land with the culture of Heaven and influence it with Kingdom Manifestations! The apostolic church has much work ahead! The Ox Anointing is required to lead and plow into the next move of the Spirit. We are called and chosen to pioneer this epic movement in church history! For those servant-leaders who are on the Lord's side, these are exciting times to be alive on planet earth!

We may be asked by the Lord to do prophetic acts that will be some of the greatest expressions of faith to reveal explosions of His Almightiness! We must pray for fresh fire and fresh anointing to destroy the yokes of bondage off the citizens in our territory.

A new breed of Kingdom Leaders will now emerge with great love and great hate, loving what God loves and hating what He hates. They will be clothed will the zeal of the Lord, fully armored, overcoming the evilest, darkest works in our day! They will slay giants with one hand while spoiling their tents with the other! Great grace, great faith, and great joy will rest upon them, empowering them to be as bold as a lion, yet meek as a lamb!

We must release restraining orders against all kinds of evil—drug lording, witchcraft, pornography, religion, political corruption, disease, and the list goes on. The hand of the Lord will be against our enemies as we take our cities for King Jesus!

Awake, Awake, oh Zion, put on your strength, put on your royal garments! Rise up from the dust of carnality, shake yourself and arise and sit in your seats of authority. Put on your kingly crowns, take your royal scepters, and put on the full armor of God! Remove the chains of slavery, rise up, sons of God. Break forth in joy, break forth into singing, for thy redemption draws nigh! The Lord shall make bare His Holy Arm in the eyes of all nations! All the ends of the earth shall see His salvation! And Kings shall come at your rising, the wealth of the world shall come unto you!

Now is the time, the set time, for the KINGS TO ARISE in their cities!

Preface

Imagine The City of God

Imagine a city where opportunities start at birth, and where children are born into greatness.

Imagine a city where children go to Kingdom schools, then Kingdom Universities obtaining a higher education in Christ.

Imagine a city where opportunities fill the atmosphere, and the city is filled with Kingdom businesses and entrepreneurs.

Imagine a city where praise, worship, and prayer fill the city like birds singing from the trees in the springtime.

Imagine a city where the crime rate is the lowest in their nation, prison cells are empty, and the streets are filled with joy and laughter.

Imagine a city where prejudice, hatred, and poverty are only taught in schools as history lessons.

Imagine a city where equal opportunity and well-paying jobs attract men and women from neighboring communities.

Imagine a city where arts and entertainment glorify God and give true creative expression of the Kingdom of Heaven upon the earth.

Imagine a city where drug addicts, prostitutes, and alcoholics are part of the redeemed community and now live as vessels of honor in God's Holy Kingdom.

Imagine a city where poverty-stricken areas are now restored, revived, and prosperous with wealthy Kingdom citizens living in safe, thriving neighborhoods.

Imagine a city that was once declared a waste is now royally revived, repaired, and rebuilt.

Imagine a city where men and women from different religions and nationalities dream of moving to the city, because they have heard it is a place where dreams come true.

Imagine a city that flourishes with Kingdom prosperity, righteousness, peace, health, and joy in the Holy Ghost.

Imagine a city where leaders from nations come to find the secrets of its growing success and prosperity.

Imagine a city so prosperous and fruitful that the Lord heals the land with abundance and prospers it to send resources to hurting nations.

Imagine a city that looks so much like Heaven, the residents experience days of Heaven upon the earth.

Imagine a city, whose citizens have awakened to righteousness, and where the glory of God exudes the atmosphere like the scent of a rose garden.

Imagine a city where hospitals are empty because there is not one sick or feeble among the people.

Imagine a city where people live as Priests and Kings making all their enemies their footstools.

Imagine a city where the Almighty God calls it His abode, His resting place, His habitation, and His home.

Imagine a city where the royal citizens of the city have made Jesus Christ King and Lord of all.

Imagine a city that looks like Goshen, radiates like Eden, and is the greatest city to live in and raise your family.

Imagine a city that the Lord calls His city, and that city is **YOUR CITY**.

YOU ARE CHOSEN AND CALLED TO CHANGE THE COURSE OF YOUR CITY!

Endorsements for The Ethos Initiative

"The Ethos Initiative offers an excellent compilation of historical and scriptural accounts humanized with Dr. Kauffman's personal experiences and observations of the Lord's desires and intents to establish His Kingdom of Heaven on the Earth. He is now sounding a clarion call to His Awake Kingdom servant leaders to assemble and congregate to share His roadmap and implement His plans to manifest the light of His governing Kingdom of Heaven on the Earth to displace the governing Kingdom of Darkness on the Earth beginning NOW."

- **Dr. Gary L. Sorensen, Professor of Abundance, Kingdom International University**

"I am so honored and blessed to be able to share my thoughts and recommendations on this powerful masterpiece. After more than fifty years of ministry all over the United States and Canada, I have met and been friends with and known hundreds of anointed men and women of God. These precious ones have carried the mantle of Apostle and Prophet and other titles given by God. These precious ones all seem to have one common denominator. They all have been given dreams or visions or destiny by God to fulfill in their ministry. However, one thing is lacking.... and this is what I want them to see and know revealed in this powerful and timely book. There has been a disconnect between vision/dream given by God and the plan or method to accomplish the bringing of the Kingdom of God to fullness in the earth and to their respective cities!! I believe the information shared in this book has been born in the Spirit and birthed in the heart of Apostle Mark Kauffman for such a time as this!! This is a spiritual and practical connection to bring into existence the vision of your ministry and the fulfillment of what God wants to accomplish with your ministry. Put this writing into practice with a servant's heart and see the majesty of God come alive in your ministry dream! Many blessings to you as we walk into this magnificent day of our Lord!!"

- **Prophet Gary Gatlin**

"In Dr. Mark Kauffman's book, *The Ethnos Initiative:Releasing the Destiny of Cities*, I hear the Holy Spirit speaking that revival and reformation will be united, married, and inseparable UNTIL we see their culmination producing a Great Awakening in the cities of our world. There will be many reformers sent to the marketplace to disciple and teach the nations as they convert to Christ and the spiritual glue in discipleship will seal and not come apart but will produce Strong Davidic warriors that will tear down the wicked, giant strongholds in the territories and rule over them through apostolic authority and prophetic vision. I hear Apostle Mark saying, 'This is the year to see the walls and veils of the enemy removed so that breakthrough will take place for all those who have persevered in spiritual warfare and that apostolic advancement is taking place in our communities for this is the year of Apostolic Advancement and Spiritual Climate Change. If the CLIMATE that we create is sustained it becomes a BELIEF SYSTEM where GOOD strongholds are exchanged for bad strongholds which can influence a whole region and create a culture of revival fire and pure reformation. This year we will see the healing of the Lord in operation to bring forth multi-cultural and multiethnic backgrounds together in unity. It is the year to RECOVER ALL.'

It is the KAIROS TIME for the Apostles and Prophets to work together and establish new foundations for transformation in our cities and countries and take dominion over them. Let us go in and possess the land. Dr. Mark reveals the secret of infiltrating our cities with apostolic government so as to change the culture that we may manifest the Kingdom of God on Earth as it is in Heaven. This is an excellent read!"

-   Dr. Timothy L. Colisino, Prophet to the Nations

"The Ethos Initiative exposes the collective Ekklesia mobilization to recover the cities and land for our owner and creator God and its battle between the usurper egregore of satan. It Is marvelous to see the reality of God's Kingdom of believers beginning to align their God-given assignments to clarify and reveal the way God's love can change the world. This will enable those still in satan's grip to see the reality of the light that Jesus is in the current fallen dark world and wake up to the fact that there are two kingdoms, and they are in the wrong one and need to get into the only eternal Kingdom of God. Once we, via God's plan, can demonstrate the abundance of the new Kingdom globally, those who God knew about at creation can step over the kingdom boundary and be with Him. The idea of church as a "kingdom government" agency is a big step towards the new paradigm of the body of Christ (church) being the economic, political, and spiritual, pivotal enterprise. The kingdom Castle (actually New Castle) is in conflict with those outside who "choose" not to belong to God. The mountains as such must be fully taken over (economically) and as in all God's battle those who are not for Him are against Him and must be removed. For example, we need to all know that we are all being told the whole truth in the media for our decisions to be sound. Excellent work, well done Dr. Mark Kauffman—

again a thoroughly sound explanation and worthy of making the time to read and digest and add to any Kingdom of God library."

- **Dr. Stan Jeffery FRSN, Founder of New Kingdom Global in Sydney, Australia**

In "The Ethos Initiative: Releasing the Destiny of Cities," Dr. Mark Kauffman delivers a powerful message that resonates with believers and leaders alike. Drawing from biblical wisdom and contemporary insight, Dr. Kauffman unveils the keys to developing leadership that can shake the very foundations of our cities. Through compelling passages like Jeremiah 22:29 and Deuteronomy 28:13, Dr. Kauffman reminds us of the divine purpose inherent in every city. With clarity and conviction, he challenges the church to rise up as catalysts for transformation, emphasizing that our help comes not from earthly institutions but from the Lord Himself.

By highlighting the power of a committed minority to shape culture, Dr. Kauffman inspires readers to take action in their communities. He shows how even a small remnant can usher in profound change, echoing the teachings of the Bible and the lessons of history. With a call to reclaim our cities for God, Dr. Kauffman underscores the importance of spiritual authority in every sphere of society. He challenges pastors and leaders to embrace their role in shaping the destiny of their communities, emphasizing the need for kingdom-minded initiatives like The Ethos Initiative.

Through insightful reflections on scripture and practical applications for today's world, "The Ethos Initiative" offers a roadmap for cultural renewal. Dr. Kauffman's passion for seeing cities transformed shines through every page, making this book a must-read for anyone committed to making a difference in their community.

Join the movement today and discover how you can help release your city's destiny through "The Ethos Initiative."

- **Dr. Larry G. Langston, International Pastor, Blessed Hope Christian Community Churches Int'l.**

Chapter 1: God Has Called Us to Cities

"O earth, earth, earth, hear the word of the LORD." - Jeremiah 22:29 KJV

This passage speaks of geographical locations. Our cities know the word of the Lord over it and can also hear the prophetic word of the Lord spoken into it. Every city has a redemptive purpose and a calling upon it. A clarion call is going out to the church from the Lord to take our place as catalytic city reformers. The destiny of our cities is in our hands. Our help in this season will not come from the White House or the Courthouse but from the Lord's House.

Culture is defined by small groups of change-agents. It only takes 3% or less of the people to shift the atmosphere and the culture of a city. What the majority believes is irrelevant; it only matters who is influencing at the TOP! Less than 3,000 people have defined the culture of world civilizations since 600 B.C. leading up to our current day. There's been roughly 22 billion people between that time frame. It will only take a small remnant to transform the current culture of our society.

And the LORD shall make thee the head, and not the tail; and thou shalt be above only, and thou shalt not be beneath; if that thou hearken unto the commandments of the Lord thy God, which I command thee this day, to observe and to do them. - Deuteronomy 28:13 KJV

The Jews teach their children this passage in Deuteronomy at a very young age. The Jewish community has trained their children to lead from the top. The Lord is about to make a cultural statement through His Ekklesia into our cities. We have large churches in America, but no governing voices. The call to transform our cities is based upon God's calling, not the size of our church. Your city needs to be a governing city. Sending people forth into every sphere of society is our present assignment.

Defining Ekklesia

The church is in transition; we currently have 40,000 denominations worldwide. We see 40,000 denomi-NATIONS (plural). But St. Peter said we are a HOLY-NATION (singular). Jesus says, "I'll build my Ekklesia (singular) and the gates of hell will not prevail against it."

Jesus prayed to the Father that we may all be one as the Father and He are one and that we also may be one in the Father and the Son. This was so the world would believe that the Father sent the Son. Yet, instead of being one, we are the most divided entity in the world.

We have 149 churches here in Lawrence County, Pennsylvania. From the book of Acts they planted one church in a city. In New Castle alone we have over 50 churches. Jamaica has more churches per square mile than can be found in any other country. Although it contains 1600 churches, it has the highest murder rate in the world. The word church is not translated from the word Ekklesia. Jesus specifically said that upon this rock, He would build His Ekklesia, not His church. Ekklesia is the original word that should've been kept, but the word was deliberately mistranslated by the authority of King James. At the very least, it should've been translated as an assembly or congregation. Ekklesia, simply stated, means to be called out! The Ekklesia was an arm of the Roman government at that present time. However, the term Ekklesia was operative in public affairs long before the Romans ever decided to use that term. While Ekklesia was not a

Christian term in those days, the concept was known and in practice for hundreds of years. The meaning of Ekklesia was commonly understood by everyone in Jesus' day. When the religious elite, government officials, or anybody heard the mention of Ekklesia they understood what it meant and its purpose; it was simply a called-out assembly.

The Ekklesia was a governing council that established policies, passed legislation, conferred/denied citizenship, and elected officials. The Ekklesia had ruling powers. When Jesus declared that He would build His Ekklesia, He knew exactly the implications of that word and its meaning. Jesus surely knew that the Ekklesia was the ruling and governing body of that day.

Thayer's Lexicon says Ekklesia means: "an assembly of the people convened at a public place for counsel and for the purpose of deliberating." So, in this hour we're leaving church as we've known it and becoming the Ekklesia. That doesn't mean we're leaving our buildings. We're just creating a new wineskin and paradigm of thinking for how the church is to operate in our present world.

The church of Jesus Christ is the governing Body of Christ in the earth to establish and demonstrate the Kingdom of God. Having been granted the authority to govern all aspects of life, they are called out and chosen by God to steward the Kingdom of God upon the earth. Our culture is shaped by the seven mountains of cultural influence that include business, government, media, arts and entertainment, education, family, and religion. Here Isaiah describes the eighth mountain, representing God's Kingdom, that will rise above all seven mountains to govern them.

And it shall come to pass in the last days, that the mountain of the Lord's house shall be established in the top of the mountains and shall be exalted above the hills; and all nations shall flow unto it. - Isaiah 2:2

Jesus gave His disciples the keys of the Kingdom of Heaven and expected the authority of His Ekklesia to far exceed the authority of the earthly Ekklesia. As an authorized Ekklesia, they bind and loose on earth anything that is already bound and loosed in Heaven. Bind and loose are legal terms. The Ekklesia that the Lord is building in our day is a divine ruling and governing body of believers formed to impact the earth from Heaven as SENT ONES.

Then said Jesus to them again, Peace be unto you: as my Father hath sent me, even so send I you. - John 20:21 KJV

The mandate upon us all is "Thy Kingdom come, and Thy will be done in Earth as it is in Heaven." As we see the restoration of the Ekklesia into the earth, it will be earmarked by supernatural manifestations, signs, wonders, spiritual immunity, and divine protection.

And he said unto them, "Go ye into all the world, and preach the gospel to every creature. He that believeth and is baptized shall be saved; but he that believeth not shall be damned. And these signs shall follow them that believe; In my name shall they cast out devils; they shall speak with new tongues; They shall take up serpents; and if they drink any deadly thing, it shall not hurt them; they shall lay hands on the sick, and they shall recover. So then after the Lord had spoken unto them, he was received up into heaven, and sat on the right hand of God. And they went forth, and preached every where, the Lord working with them, and confirming the word with signs following. Amen". - Mark 16:15-20

Ninety-seven percent of the Saints don't belong in the pulpit. They belong in the seven mountains of influence. We are citizens of the Kingdom of Heaven, and that Kingdom is meant to be in every sphere. They said of the early church, "These people are everywhere!" Only the Kingdom of God can move into the culture and bring transformation. Islam cannot do that, they don't have solutions only a religion. Religion complains, confronts, and criticizes, but has no answers. To bring solutions we need the wisdom and anointing of the Holy Ghost. The Holy Ghost is the source for cultural transformation. As the Ekklesia is restored, we will see the dislodging of demonic strongholds in individuals and over territories. Where these demonic strongholds once existed and ruled, there will be the release of the manifested presence and power of the Lord.

In the book of Acts, Stephen called Moses and the Israelites the Ekklesia in the wilderness. When they came out of Egypt and camped at Mount Sinai the Lord restored His Kingdom government back into the earth. The Commandments were the governing laws for this chosen priesthood and new holy nation. Under this canopy of the newly formed administration and government there was not one sick or feeble among them, exemplifying spiritual immunity. Everyone prospered as the Ekklesia, even Manasseh, the smallest of all the tribes.

The True Church of Jesus Christ

Now there was long war between the house of Saul and the house of David: but David waxed stronger and stronger, and the house of Saul waxed weaker and weaker. - 2 Samuel 3:1 KJV

The church at large is becoming weaker and weaker. But the remnant church (the apostolic/prophetic church) is becoming stronger and stronger, increasingly better and better. The earmarks of this Ekklesia in the coming days will be the nature of God (love). Every saint has a ministry and ministry is touching people. We touch people with God's love. Worship should express God's love. Every healing expresses God's love. Every teaching should express God's love. Every conversation should express God's love. Salvation and Deliverance are the results of God's love.

Radical paradigm shifts are taking place in the church. By the year 2030 you will not recognize the carnal church, nor will you recognize the spiritual church. Mega church is over! They may not close their doors tomorrow, but the Kingdom has been taken from them. Saul remained on the throne, but the Kingdom left him for another. Entertainment-based churches will die out by 2030. This is the Kingdom at war, not Hollywood. We are shifting from performance church to prophetic church. It's not a comforting gospel but a confronting gospel. The question is, are we exciting the people or are we igniting the people? This next move is about transformation of culture, not growing our churches.

Billy Graham was a God-given celebrity, Kathryn Kuhlman was a well-renowned celebrity, Aimee Semple McPherson was a notable celebrity in God's Kingdom. In this next move God is going to raise up a new breed of celebrities— men and women who walk in true humility. Now your religious mind immediately says, 'Oh no, God wouldn't do that." The word celebrity simply means "a famous and well-known person." The Bible said the fame of Jesus went throughout the land. Jesus was a celebrity. God's raising up a new breed of Kingdom celebrities who will be known for their influence, not their egomania. But they will be known for reshaping culture as we know it. They will be known for the signs and wonders that follow them. They will be celebrated for their deeds of love and compassion. They will be known for building a new society called the Kingdom of Heaven, a Kingdom of righteousness, peace, joy, and love. And there will be a group that works with them known as a faceless generation. The Earth may not know who they are, but heaven knows them, and so do the powers of darkness. This faceless generation is fearfully and wonderfully made and will give hell a really bad day every day.

The true church of Jesus Christ has been sent into the planet as ambassadors of heaven, to bring Kingdom colonization and influence every sphere of society. They will plant the heavens into the Earth, and will, in their lifetime, see days of heaven upon the Earth.

And I have put my words in thy mouth, and I have covered thee in the shadow of mine hand, that I may plant the heavens, and lay the foundations of the earth, and say unto Zion, Thou art my people. - Isaiah 51:16 KJV

And thou shalt write them upon the door posts of thine house, and upon thy gates: that your days may be multiplied, and the days of your children, in the land which the LORD sware unto your fathers to give them, as the days of heaven upon the earth. - Deuteronomy 11:20-21 KJV

Cities Have a Destiny

Our cities must now become an open heaven, and a governing seat for King Jesus. It's time to make principalities and powers suffer for what they have done to our cities. Where you have physical authority, you have spiritual authority (you must define to which part of the city you are called). Which of these seven mountains of society are you assigned to: business, government, media, arts and entertainment, education, the family, and religion? For example, if you are a pastor you're called to at least one mountain and that is the family mountain.

From the beginning, God's intention was to bless cities and nations, not just individuals. He is the God of Nations.

Go then and make disciples of all the nations, baptizing them into the name of the Father and of the Son and of the Holy Spirit. - Matthew 28:19 AMPC

The King James version more accurately states, "Go ye therefore, and teach all nations." We are not called to just disciple people, but to disciple nations and cities. Cities are groaning to be released into their destiny and calling. They're crying out to be ushered into the fullness of God's blueprint and into His Kingdom purposes.

We know that everything in the universe is still in great pain now. Everything cries together in pain, like a woman who is ready to have a baby. - Romans 8:22 EASY

The King James declares, "All creation is groaning." The majority of the church is waiting for God to do something. Meanwhile, He's waiting on us to do something! He's waiting for you and me to get engaged Monday through Saturday in the marketplace, where we work and live.

And when the LORD saw that he turned aside to see, God called unto him out of the midst of the bush, and said, Moses, Moses. And he said, Here am I. And he said, Draw not nigh hither: put off thy shoes from off thy feet, for the

23

place whereon thou standest is holy ground. - Exodus 3:4-5 KJV

Take a look at how God came to Moses's place of employment, while he was working. His livelihood was a shepherd in his father-in-law's sheep business. Why was the ground holy? Because God's presence was there. Wherever you are on Monday through Saturday is a sacred place. It's where God desires to meet you and transform the environment with the culture of heaven through you. The Lord is looking for servant-leaders, like Joseph and Daniel, on whom He can pour out a fresh anointing, a new mantle of wisdom, knowledge, understanding, and favor upon them, all so that they can bestow the Lord's blessings upon their cities. We must identify the Josephs, the Daniels, and the Esthers, equipping them and empowering them for transformation. Therefore, I have created the Ethos Initiative with keys for establishing city-shaking leadership.

Chapter 2: Your Passion Reveals Your Assignment

Pharaoh had a dream of an approaching crucible that could only be interpreted by Joseph. We must raise up Josephs, who are problem-solvers and decision-makers, able to solve life's most critical issues. Nothing is more powerful in the prophetic realm than spiritual intelligence. Like Joseph and Daniel demonstrated, this intelligence solved critical problems and released a Divine-destiny Word at a God-ordained moment.

The prophet Joel told us that in the last days our sons and daughters will prophesy. The most prophetic generation is already in the planet today. Jesus sent out 70 disciples in Matthew 28:19 and said, "Go make disciples of all nations." In specifically choosing 70 apostles, Jesus made a powerful statement. According to Genesis chapter 10, the descendants of Noah formed 70 nations. In choosing and sending 70 apostles, Jesus was revealing His purpose and plan for all nations to be blessed. Revelation 22:2 explains that the Lord has made provision for the "healing of the nations." So where do we begin such a task? We must start with healing cities in preparation to heal the nations.

We need model Kingdom cities. But where, in America, can you find a Kingdom city? The Muslims have taken over Dearborn, Michigan; the Mormons created their model in Salt Lake City, Utah; the Jews own that big rock called Manhattan, NYC. But where are the model Kingdom cities that reflect the culture of Heaven and the nature of God? The stage is set, and the world is waiting for courageous, righteous leaders to demonstrate the Kingdom of God in every sphere of society. How will we do this? Everything rises and falls on leadership. This is our finest moment.

The remnant church is at a place of convergence. This means that your life is in a position, a divine tipping point, whereby God has prepared you to bring cultural transformation through your giftings, wisdom, anointings, favor, resources, and spiritual intellect.

In scripture, there was a unique tribe that always knew what to do, and when to do it. They had such perception and wisdom that an entire nation listened to them and followed their lead. They were called the Sons of Issachar.

And of the children of Issachar, which were men that had understanding of the times, to know what Israel ought to do; the heads of them were two hundred; and all their brethren were at their commandment. - 1 Chronicles 12:32 KJV

To understand the times is the Prophetic edge; knowing what to do is the Apostolic edge. *Understanding the times* is the ability to scan the heavens and see and know what God is doing. *Knowing what to do* is the practical application of taking what God is saying and doing in the heavens and then planting it in the Earth.

And I have put my words in thy mouth, and I have covered thee in the shadow of mine hand, that I may plant the heavens, and lay the foundations of the earth, and say unto Zion, Thou art my people. - Isaiah 51:16 KJV

The Church of Jesus Christ must create a new narrative that is fueled by hope!

Hope deferred makes the heart sick: But when the desire cometh, it is a tree of life. - Proverbs 13:12 KJV

To create such a narrative, you must discover who are the visionaries. We are desperate for visionary leaders in our world today. We must forge new partnerships and alliances with key Kingdom leaders within our cities, uniting together, to create divine synergy for apostolic thrust and city transformation. The question is, will you be part of these apostolic prophetic teams that the Lord is presently raising up, who will transform our cities and culture? As Kingdom citizens, we must be united and mobilized to be force-multipliers and change-agents at the forefront of culture.

Unity is not sameness but diversity. Your theology is not going to always align one with another. But you're born on the planet to merge as one for a CAUSE. And you will need to define that cause. What's your role that you will play? What is your assignment that complements the CAUSE? Like David on the battlefield ready to fight Goliath, we must understand there is a cause, a purpose, for every battle we face in our present world.

And David said, "What have I now done? Is there not a cause?" - 1 Samuel 17:29 KJV

My son, Christian Mark, was raised in the Kingdom of God to know that he has a purpose, a cause in life, whereby he will make a difference, and be an influencer in his world. As a result, he's had multiple interviews in the sports industry. Teams who have conversed with him are the San Antonio Spurs, the Cleveland Cavaliers, the Indiana Pacers, and the Philadelphia 76ers. All have all had great interest in working with my son. Between his junior and senior year over the summer, he will be interning for the New York Knicks.

Christian Mark completed a dissertation on LinkedIn about how to succeed at pursuing a job in the sports industry. He's had almost 20,000 views. I prophesied to him in the coming days that he will write a book to empower men and women going into his field. Realizing he has an anointing and favor upon his life, he understands the power of preparation and hard work. HIS PASSION IS EXEMPLARY AND HIS PASSION HAS REVEALED HIS ASSIGNMENT.

He knows his assignment, who he is, what he has, and his purpose for being in the planet. Since he was five years old, he has prepared for this. As a little boy, preparing to go to school every morning, he did not watch cartoons on the television. Instead, he watched Sports Center and ESPN daily sports news in preparation for his purpose. Preparation is never wasted.

What's your passion? It reveals your assignment! What are you doing to prepare for your assignment? The early church was filled with passionate people. Some of you may have lost your passion and need to get it back. You may need to recover your first love with Jesus.

For if by one man's offence death reigned by one; much more they which receive abundance of grace and of the gift of righteousness shall reign in life by one, Jesus Christ. - Romans 5:17 KJV.

To reign simply means to change things. God is inviting us to co-labor with Him whereby, we will initiate God's Kingdom Culture as we invade our cities.

And he called his ten servants, and delivered them ten pounds, and said unto them, Occupy till I come. - Luke 19:13 KJV

The king was happy and said to his servant, "You have done well. You are a good servant that I can trust. You have used a small amount of money well. So now you will rule over ten cities."
- Luke 19:17 EASY

In this parable, the Lord is teaching us the principles for how we can rule our cities.
- *You have done well* - speaks of the spirit of excellence.
- *You are a good servant* - speaks of a high level of servanthood.
- *I can trust you* - represents a spirit of faithfulness.
- *Faithful in small things* - represents preparation, and qualification for larger things.

We are in the midst of an amazing new "Renaissance Era," which is the convergence of a multitude of technologies, business models, humanitarian outreaches, new, innovative ideas, and new ministry strategies. Through these, we expand the effectiveness of our ministries into our cities. God is calling us to be wall-less churches. It was said of the early church, "these people were everywhere!" They influenced every sphere of society. That cannot be over emphasized in this season. The churches that will succeed in this season will become wall-less, meaning doing more than meeting inside a walled-up church every Sunday.

Let's me give you a list of what we are doing at Jubilee Ministries International in New Castle, Pennsylvania that moves the church beyond the four walls to become a wall-less church:

- The NOW Project - feeding over 1,500 families every month.

- We are on Dominion TV - reaching 170 nations.
- We are on Faith TV - reaching 8.5 million homes in America.
- We steward the Christian Chamber of Commerce of Pennsylvania - for current business owners and aspiring entrepreneurs.
- INK publishing company - we publish books for fivefold leaders.
- International Network of Kingdom Leaders - empowering leaders around the world.
- The Royal Kingdom Academy - weekly equipping the saints to be a wall-less church.
- The Man Cave - empowering men to man up, taking their rightful place in their home, local church, and in their city.
- Virtuous Women Meetings - equipping and empowering women to fulfill their designed destiny.
- The Jr. Man Cave - igniting young men for purpose.
- Harvest Parties for Children in the community - including a host of other programs for our children.
- Jubilee Ministries International serves multiple businesses, hosted in our city; Metrovitalization, Kingdom Couture, Regulus Energy, Sovereign Martial Arts Worldwide, Kingdom Green Energy, Focus Life Institute, Flowers Masonry, Butz Flowers and Gifts, and The LW Collective –just name a few.
- Last, but not least, we are launching the Kingdom International University - already in thirty nations, we are fully accredited. Our dream is to have a campus in every nation in the world.

Commissioned by Encounters

Most importantly, as we discuss releasing the destiny within our cities, we must lead our cities into an encounter with God. We owe the world an encounter with Jesus! As we lead our communities into these encounters with the Lord, the people in our cities will receive fresh commissioning into the new thing that God is wanting to do within that place. God always commissions people by encounters. Here are a few biblical examples that demonstrate this principle:

- Moses encountered God in a burning bush, and then was commissioned to deliver the Israelites from the cruel tyranny of Pharaoh.
- Joshua encountered the Captain of the Host where he received his commissioning. He led the children of Israel through the Jordan River and into the Promised Land.
- Gideon encountered the Angel of the Lord; his encounter turned him into another man from cowardly to courageous! He was commissioned to lead his army of 300 into the battle victoriously, defeating the Midianites.
- The Apostle Paul was also commissioned by encounter on the road to Damascus where he abandoned murdering Christians and persecuting the church. Thrusting him into his dynamic role of an apostle and early church leader, he wrote most of the New Testament.

Therefore, we should be praying for an outpouring of the Holy Spirit within our cities. Then fresh encounters will take place within our churches, our schools, inside government buildings, in our business district, in our neighborhoods, and in our homes. God will commission people for Kingdom work in conjunction with revealing their passions and assignments. As a result, our cities will never be the same as the people within live out their God-given destinies!

Chapter 3: We've Never Come This Way Before

It's time to step off the map. In the words of Joshua, "We have never come this way before." We have no maps for this new season and our forefathers can't help us. We must depend on the compass of the Holy Spirit. Do we have any risk-takers here ready to pioneer the way?

City churches must be created to empower and mobilize the Church for societal change.
Every church must become an empowerment center! Power is given for one reason and one reason alone: to give it away. We can no longer pastor our congregants to only maintain their salvation. Most American churches solely operate as maintenance centers.

Ask of me, and I shall give thee the heathen for thine inheritance, And the uttermost parts of the earth for thy possession. - Psalm 2:8 KJV.

This is our present apostolic mandate. This is the call: to invade society and colonize it with a Kingdom of Heaven. Why do you come to church? We do not come to church for an emotional fix, but to receive a renewed mind. Exchanging our minds for God's mind, we can have the mind of Christ. Secular education gives you information, language, recognition, and not language comprehension. An example is that although you may learn English, you will not learn what it means. They don't understand or teach what decoding is. Recognition should lead to comprehension and then comprehension should lead to application that ultimately leads to manifestation! When the world was perishing, God did not send a breakthrough angel. No, He sent His Word. His Word is settled in the heavens, and that is wonderful, but it needs to be established in the Earth! How do you establish the word in your earth? Job said, "Thou shalt decree a thing, and it shall be established unto you."

An urgent mandate is upon the apostolic church of Jesus Christ to rise up and impact the territories where we live by transforming the current infrastructure and the culture of our cities, counties, and states. This is Kingdom transformation. The time has arrived for us to reclaim our cities and states for King Jesus. How do we do this? By influencing every sphere of society with a new Kingdom culture, we will bring societal change and will secure God's Presence in our cities, states, and nation for generations to come.

The Welsh Revival in 1904-1905 was led by young man named Evan Roberts. As wonderful as this great move was in the nation of Wales, it was weak in that it only evangelized the nation, but it failed to transform it and disciple new believers. One hundred twenty years later, Wales is a very dark nation and less than 5% of the nation claims to be Christians. After the revival over 85% of the Welsh people had given their life to Christ. What did they do wrong? They did not disciple the nation, but only evangelized the nation of Wales. They did not take the gospel of the Kingdom and influence religion, government, economics, or the educational system.

Just over 60 years ago the church was the most influential entity in America that defined culture. Now, we are at the bottom of the list, while the media has risen to number one. Indeed, many paradigm shifts are underway across America that include shifts in culture, government, family and in economic spheres. But regrettably, the church has been absent from most of these changes. Many good things are happening in America, but good does not equate to righteous.

We are presently in a battle for cities, our state, and nation. God's Kingdom policies are not determined by the media or by governments, but by Jesus and His Ekklesia. My state of Pennsylvania is important to what God is doing in this hour; we are the keystone state, the catalyst for the apostolic movement. It's important as leaders that we know God's original purpose and intent for our cities and states. Every city and state have a destiny.

In this season we employ a displacing mentality. Church is no longer just a religious edifice. Although my wife and I have pastored Jubilee Ministries International for 35 years, we think of our church as a Kingdom government agency.

Pennsylvania is called to be a creative and governing force in this nation. Because of this reality, we must re-occupy our state. Every city and every state have a unique DNA and inheritance. Pennsylvania's DNA is prophetic, apostolic, and governmental. We must know the destiny upon your city. The Lord wants to raise up pillars in the city, He wants to raise a bastion. A bastion is a person strongly defending and upholding principles, attitudes, and activities. It's time to build bastion leaders. My wife and I have been graced by the Lord to build such fiery leaders who won't back down!

Prophetically, we must understand the times and know the heart and mind of God for the season in which we live. Apostolically, we must create solutions and strategies for reformation. We must change our cities and transform them for the glory of God in our lifetime.

America is now in a modern Civil War. The nation is divided. The Apostle Paul said, "Of course there must be divisions among you so that God's approval will be recognized." Division is for recognition. Much like Elijah at Mount Carmel, the nation of Israel was divided; some served Jehovah and others served Baal. It was during that tension and division that divine recognition of who was sovereign, and Lord of All was revealed and manifested. The fire and glory of Heaven came amid hostility.

Currently, the environment is right and it's ripe for a move of God. The Lord always does His finest work in the midst of a pagan society. We have now entered a new level of warfare to capture the culture and transform it. As in the days of Elijah, so is it in our day! We are beginning to see two kingdoms collide: the Kingdom of God and the kingdom of darkness. It will be a head on collision, but light always swallows up darkness because the greater always swallows up the lesser. Greater is He that is in us.

The kingdoms of this world are become the kingdoms of our Lord and of his Christ, and he shall reign forever and ever! - Revelation 11:15

The church has always thrived in the middle of a pagan society. It's time to act as God's chosen people. The First Commission in Scripture was Genesis 1:26, "Let them have dominion." And that call for dominion has never changed. As an army of the Lord, we cannot remain silent. The Ekklesia of God must respond to the call and assemble for such a time as this. Let them have dominion. It's a law! There will be a generation that says, "Be it unto me, according to your word, Lord." What is your response to the call?

Chapter 4: God's Kingdom Government

Thy Kingdom come! Jesus did not come to bring a religion, but a government called the Kingdom of Heaven. When Kingdom government is restored, based upon the corporate anointing of Psalm 133, it will release God's commanded blessings over the citizens of our cities and state.

Behold, how good and how pleasant it is For brethren to dwell together in unity! It is like the precious ointment upon the head, that ran down upon the beard, Even Aaron's beard: That went down to the skirts of his garments; As the dew of Hermon, And as the dew that descended upon the mountains of Zion: For there the LORD commanded the blessing, Even life for evermore.
- Psalm 133:1-3 KJV

Presently, we have government officials trying to run a planet that they don't own. "The earth is the Lord's and the fullness there of" and "the government is upon the shoulders of Jesus Christ and His Ekklesia."

The book of the generation of Jesus Christ, the son of David, the son of Abraham. - Matthew 1:1 KJV

This is also a Davidic and Abrahamic calling. As the seed of David, we are promised the throne and as the seed of Abraham we are promised the earth. The earth is the Lord's, and the throne is the right to rule it.

The Earth belongs to God! Everything in all the world is his! - Psalms 24:1 TLB

And the seventh angel sounded; and there were great voices in heaven, saying, The kingdoms of this world are

become the kingdoms of our Lord, and of his Christ; and he shall reign for ever and ever. - Revelation 11:15

The systems of this world will become the systems of our God and of his Christ. It is our endeavor to transform the kingdoms of this world and their systems into the Kingdoms of our God and of His Christ.

Dr. Myles Monroe gives us a clear definition of the Kingdom of God: "A kingdom is the governing influence of a king over his territory, impacting it with his personal will, purpose, and intent, producing a culture, values, morals, and a lifestyle that reflect the king's desire and nature for his citizens." The Kingdom is where God's perfect will and his perfect rule is done in the earth, as it is in heaven, through the church of Jesus Christ.

Thy kingdom come. Thy will be done in earth, as it is in heaven. - Matthew 6:10 KJV

In chapter 6 of my book *Kings Arise*, I described the Greek definition of kingdom:

> In the Greek, kingdom is the word, BASILEIA, which means sovereignty, royal Power, and Dominion. Vine's dictionary defines the word as royalty and rule, stemming from the root word that is rendered as 'walk or foot.' The Kingdom of God is a walk, a lifestyle that we live and demonstrate in our present world.

It does not come just alone in word, but in power.

...for the kingdom of God is not in word, but in power. - 1 Corinthians 4:20

It's not to be confused as an event or a coming attraction in the future. The kingdom is within you right now as righteousness, peace, and joy in the Holy Ghost. The Lord Jesus Christ desires that His people take the governing influence of the Kingdom and affect the spiritual and natural spheres of the seven mountains in our society. We accomplish this by being salt and light.

Ye are the salt of the earth: but if the salt have lost his savour, wherewith shall it be salted? It is thenceforth good for nothing, but to be cast out, and to be trodden under foot of men. Ye are the light of the world. A city that is set on an hill cannot be hid. - Matthew 5:13-14

On the day of Pentecost, Jesus gave the 120 men and women power. He declared them witnesses both in Jerusalem, in Judea, in Samaria, and the uttermost parts of the Earth. It began with having authority over the region. Once they influenced their region, then they could go beyond. What is God's heartbeat for your city? We write the vision down, articulate it, and then make it plain for others to understand. It's time that we mobilize and unify the key leaders within our cities. We have a godly agenda of "Thy Kingdom come; thy will be done in earth as it is in heaven." We are not here to back political parties, but to advance and establish the Kingdom of God! We are not an arm of any party! We're the voice of influence in Christ's Kingdom! We are the arm and an extension of Heaven's government.

Chapter 5: Kingdom Gatekeepers

...thy seed shall possess the gate of thine enemies. - Genesis 22:17b

In Biblical times, elders judged the gates and resolved disputes; they were called judges or magistrates. They examined everything coming in and out of the city. Anything unlawful was arrested and dealt with at the gates. The gates of a city are where the mind molders shape the culture of society within a city. These are the 8 gates shaping the mind and culture of today's world: 1) media 2) education 3) government 4) religious 5) law 6) financial 7) cultural and 8) business.

These are different from the seven mountains. We see the family, sports and entertainment are not gates; they are mountains. It is our responsibility to show up at the gates with a displacing mentality. The first thing that Jesus said about His church that He would build was, "The gates of Hades shall not prevail against it" (Matthew 16:18). The gates represented the demonic powers that ruled over the cities from the spirit realm. Those powers, through different kinds of human agencies, controlled everything that came into the city, spiritually speaking. Dominating the city, they permitted what could occur legally, socially, politically, and economically.

At this present time, these gates are being governed by demonic powers through human beings that have yielded to these evil powers at the gates of the city. These gates are meant to be governed by God's apostolic people. For decades, the powers of darkness have dominated our cities across America and around the world. Unoccupied and unprotected gates make cities, counties, and states vulnerable to wicked ruling entities. To be authentic, every move of God must penetrate all spheres of society. We have moved from just hosting revivals to introducing an apostolic reformation of society.

I don't have a problem with revivals, but this next move is bigger than revival. Revival was meant to wake up the dead. But Kingdom Reformation changes the landscapes of our communities with the culture of Heaven. This apostolic reformation requires gatekeepers positioned within a city, to judge the gates and resolve disputes.

Decades ago, satan took control of these gates, to dominate our cities for his purposes. His occupancy, in most cases, is almost total. In order for the Kingdom of God to come to our cities in the same Pentecostal power as the first century church, we must learn to recover these gates from the enemies' hands and cast down their ruling spirits.

In Matthew chapter 16, "binding and loosing" are presented as legal terms. Demons break laws because no one enforces the law. But we, as Kingdom Citizens, can pass legislation and judge their violations.

That in blessing I will bless thee, and in multiplying I will multiply thy seed as the stars of the heaven, and as the sand which is upon the sea shore; and thy seed shall possess the gate of his enemies; and in thy seed shall all the nations of the earth be blessed; because thou hast obeyed my voice. - Genesis 22:17-18 KJV

God promised Abraham that the true descendants of Abraham would possess, by faith, the gates of their enemies, reaping a mighty harvest. This promise of a great harvest **is directly linked** with taking possession of the gates that are presently in the hands of the enemy.

And they blessed Rebekah, and said unto her, Thou art our sister, be thou the mother of thousands of millions, and let thy seed possess the gate of those which hate them. - Genesis 24:60 KJV

Gate-taking was, and remains, a necessary preparation for city-taking. Once these gates are recovered, the spiritual blindness (affecting the minds of many people) will immediately be removed, and then we can bring in the harvest.

If we desire the Kingdom of God to invade our cities just like the power of the Holy Ghost invaded cities in the book of Acts, then we must learn to recover the gates from the powers of darkness and cast down the ruling entities that control the gates. We will later discuss how to create Upper Room environments and atmospheres to influence a city, a state, and a nation.

The first thing that Jesus said about the church is that He would build it, and the gates of hell would not prevail against it! The gates that Jesus spoke of were not physical gates, but rather spheres of influence and control, shaping the way people think and behave. The gates are the mind molders in a city. Responsible for indoctrinating the way people think, these gates determine how they perceive their world. After the gates shape the people's thinking, the behavior follows what their thoughts contain.

But if our gospel be hid, it is hid to them that are lost: in whom the god of this world hath blinded the minds of them which believe not, lest the light of the glorious gospel of Christ, who is the image of God, should shine unto them. For we preach not ourselves, but Christ Jesus the Lord; and ourselves your servants for Jesus' sake. For God, who commanded the light to shine out of darkness, hath shined in our hearts, to give the light of the knowledge of the glory of God in the face of Jesus Christ. - 2 Corinthians 4:3-6 KJV

In these verses, we see how the god of this world has blinded the minds of people. Hell battles to control the minds of mankind. But we have a more powerful weapon that will open darkened eyes. It is called LIGHT! First and foremost, light represents Jesus, who as the Light of the World, told His disciples, "You are the light of the world." Light also represents truth, revelation, and solutions to problems. Standing next to darkness, light always wins!

Being a sinner is easy to do but being a saint and a light to our world takes the following: discipline, sacrifice, passion, perseverance, prayer, courage and being a presence driven person. Faith, hope, and love are all expressions of light. The greatest assignment of hell against you is to turn off your light. Examine how the following spirits attempt to do this today:

- The spirit of Goliath still exists, mocking and intimidating mankind.
- The spirit of Herod is still alive today, killing our youth through abortion, murder, and drug abuse.
- The Midianite spirit is alive now, keeping God's people paralyzed in fear.
- The spirit of Pharaoh is active today, keeping people captive to their sins.
- The spirit of Jezebel exists in incarcerating men, women, boys, and girls with sexual perversion.
- The spirit of Absalom is alive and well on planet earth, dividing churches, families, and scarring relationships.

- The spirit of Nebuchadnezzar abides today, alluring people into false worship.
- The spirit of Hamon is seen now, discriminating, and dividing nationalities.
- The spirit of Baal is present today through pornography.

But there is good news! There is a spirit that is more powerful than all the spirits combined! He is called the Holy Spirit; He is the light of the world living inside of you and me! Therefore, the solutions to the above problems are here today as well:

- For every Goliath there must be a David!
- For every Herod, there must be a Jesus!
- For every Midianite, there must be a Gideon!
- For every Pharaoh, there must be a Moses!
- For every Jezebel, there must be a Jehu!
- For every Absalom, there must be a Solomon!
- For every Nebuchadnezzar, there must be three Hebrew boys!
- For every Hamon, there must be an Esther!
- For every prophet of Baal, there is an Elijah!

Traveling to and fro throughout the Earth, hell's intent is to cover up the candle that you are. It is time to uncover what has been covered—not just in the world, but in the church as well. The word of the Lord is going forth, once again saying, "Let there be light!"

Many years ago, the church fell asleep, while the enemy sowed wicked seeds in our cities, but an awakening is upon us. The true church of Jesus Christ is emerging to recover what was lost. There are also geographical locations full of demonic activity. These gates can be temples, historic

44

monuments, pornography stores, psychic centers, and buildings where false religions worship. These gates also include sites where witchcraft is practiced. Additional gates can include murder sites (like the Valentine's Day massacre in Chicago that opened up a murderous gate) and abortion clinics.

The Woke movement is a counterfeit for the AWAKE MOVEMENT. "First the natural, then the spiritual," Paul said. He will always unleash the counterfeit before God releases the authentic. There is a divine order in rebuilding and reforming a city. It begins by taking back the gates!

There have been individuals who are fully possessed by satan himself. They were possessed by a demonic principality with the ability to influence and control hundreds of thousands of people. We saw that with Napoleon, Adolf Hitler, Mussolini, and Anton Lavey, the founder of the church of satan. There are also what I call gate groups. These are groups of individuals have become a gate of hell, unleashing demonic propaganda. Freemasonry, Wicca, Mormonism, LGBTQ, The ACLU (American Civil Liberties Union), the porn industry, and Islam are examples of gate groups. While we hate what they do, we do not hate the individuals in these groups. The Scriptures tell us that we do not wrestle against flesh and blood, but against principalities and powers and spiritual wickedness in heavenly places that control the gates of influence. We must use our authority in Christ to dethrone these demonic powers and recover the gates by establishing righteousness, justice, peace, and joy.

Wokeism

Wokeism has become a new religion in America. It believes that good is evil and evil is good. The leading principle for wokeism is that every man can do what is right in his own eyes and that it's justifiable. It amazes me how they believe that anything is acceptable except the Bible. We are experiencing a direct assault on the Name of the Lord and the Word of the Lord. This new religion called Wokeism wants to silence the church, like Haman in the book of Esther. It's an outright attack to keep the church muted. Today we are in an Esther moment! We must decree God's Word in truth. We must declare the Word of the Lord into the present darkness, so the Lord can re-create the narrative. Because of Esther's voice of righteousness, a nation was saved in one day. A divine reversal took place in favor of the Jews. As the church awakens and arises by taking its rightful seat of authority, we will see the balance of power shifting our way. We will experience one divine reversal after another, for the glory of God. The church can no longer be silent. We must break our silence and declare the Word of the Lord for it is the highest authority in the universe!

You will also decide and decree a thing, and it will be established for you; And the light [of God's favor] will shine upon your ways. - Job 22:28 AMP

Wokeism is incompatible with biblical values, and if it's left unchecked, it will undermine the foundation of our American society. Wokeism originated from critical theory, which challenges existing power structures, and seeks to dismantle what we know as universal truths. It challenges the sanctity of who we are created to be by God in His likeness and image as males and females. Wokeism believes gender is a spectrum that individuals can self-determined which one they want to be. This new religion wants to control and manipulate society with their ideologies, where violence could result if people do not conform. This new religion operates in an antichrist spirit with the purpose of robbing our society of our faith in God. By destroying the systems of justice and freedom, they purpose and attempt to replace our faith with whatever ideologies they choose to live by.

But the Ekklesia of Jesus Christ must rise up by telling the truth in love. The Woke Movement refuses to accept that there is ultimate truth. That truth is person, and His name is Jesus Christ. Jesus is the way, the truth, and the life. Our responsibility, as followers of Jesus Christ, is to uphold the standard set forth by God and His Holy Word This ultimately brings righteousness, peace, and joy into our society. Many Christians are fearful of Woke, but God has not given us a spirit of fear, but love, power, and a sound mind, Presently, we are in a war that battles for the culture. As believers, the only battles we will lose are the ones we do not engage in. We overcome evil with good! The weapons of our warfare are not carnal, but they are mighty through God to the pulling down of strongholds. It's imperative that we stand for truth and speak it in love! We have a wonderful promise that the kingdoms of this world are become the kingdoms of our God and of His Christ. We are always triumphant, always victorious in Christ Jesus!

But thanks be to God, who always leads us in triumph in Christ, and through us spreads and makes evident everywhere the sweet fragrance of the knowledge of Him. - 2 Corinthians 2:14 AMP

Celebrating at the Gates

As the body of Christ is presently receiving revelation concerning the gates of our cities, most of what we have been hearing has been from the negative aspects within the gates. In most conversations, people talk about what needs to be changed at the gates. But when we are dealing with the gates of culture, we must always stop and reflect. Celebrate all the good things that are resident within those gates. It's important that we thank the Lord for the amazing things that are happening at our cities' gates. Using good discernment to determine what things should be celebrated within the gates, we simultaneously limit what things should **not** be tolerated within the gates. When we celebrate the aspects that make our cities great, the citizens of the community will join us in this praise, ushering in a spirit of unity into the community. It's important as Kingdom leaders that we find out what is resident within the gates that can be celebrated and magnify those things within the community. Celebrating these good pieces of our communities, we prophetically encourage and refocus them on all the wonderful things that we share together.

Chapter 6: Kinetic Energy

The Lord showed me that we have entered a season of divine kinetic energy. Kinetic energy is the energy that an object has when it's in motion. If you want to accelerate an object, then you must apply force. Applying force and pressure releases kinetic energy. After the process of applying force is done, energy has been transferred into the object and the object will move at an accelerated pace.

Kinetic energy is the opposite of static energy. For example, static energy is like rubbing your feet against the carpet as you walk and then getting shocked when you touch the doorknob. Applying the brakes to a car is static energy.

There is potential energy as well. Potential energy is energy that is stored in an object due to its position or condition. It's not a force, but it could be converted into kinetic energy, or energy in motion. An example would be a car sitting in neutral; the potential resides within it to move, yet it's not going anywhere. Or imagine a roller coaster being pulled up the hill by a chain; that is potential energy. However, when it goes down the hill it now is kinetic energy. Potential energy is a slow process. Climbing up that hill in the roller coaster takes forever, but once you reach the top, kinetic energy shifts into gear, and everything accelerates. Suddenly, you're moving quickly down the hill with nothing to stop you!

Kinetic force is a dynamic force. Kinetic friction forms galaxies, and all galaxies are created to move in cadence with each other. Each planet has its divine placement in that order. When two planets collide, it's called static friction. This slows down the galaxy. Symbolically, this sounds like a church split to me, or a divorce, or business partners dissolving their relationship. But kinetic friction moves with such dynamic force that it gravitates free radical objects into its orbit until they find their place in the flow. When planets are aligned and united, moving in cadence, they make other planets and meteors part of their galaxy. It becomes magnetic and everything the galaxy needs to be a galaxy is formed because of kinetic energy. As we learn to move united in cadence, everything we need will come looking for us. In this season, things are migrating towards us. Kinetic energy is what God uses to FORM a galaxy. When God does something new, He uses kinetic energy to create it. God created science and mastered it for His purposes. God is the great scientist. Even when God moves, He does so by using kinetic force.

In Acts chapter 2, there was a sound, then a rushing mighty wind, then came fire, and then they were filled with the Holy Ghost. Soon after, nations came and 3,000 got saved; that's kinetic energy. That Holy Ghost used *divine* kinetic energy to flow into the upper room. It poured out, influencing everything in its path. This kinetic outpouring attracted everything into its vortex. Kinetic energy attracts people, resources, wealth, creativity, heaven, things that have been lost, and restores what's been lost. It's magnetic in its very nature.

All it takes is for one person to create a movement. One will put 1,000 to flight, and two will put 10,000 to flight. When two galaxies collide, the dynamic friction causes the stars to gravitate to the center of the galaxy and it's called inward migration. In that natural example, I just told you how wealth transfer happens. When two galaxies collide, the greater swallows up the lesser.

As I said before, we're about to see two kingdoms collide between the Kingdom of God and the kingdom of darkness, but God's Kingdom is creating a brighter galaxy because the greater always swallows up the lesser. Greater is He that is in us! Let me confirm this by putting scripture on it.

The kingdoms of this world are become the kingdoms of our Lord and of his Christ, and he shall reign forever and ever! - Revelation 11:15

We are moving out of the season of static friction and away from the limitations of potential energy into the dynamics of kinetic energy.

Now watch this--because of divine kinetic energy, we are moving from declaration to demonstration! We are moving from proclamation to manifestation! It's a season of manifestation!

Chapter 7: Creating Atmospheres

We must recapture the atmosphere of our cities for this result:

- Atmosphere creates climate (standard, prevailing attitudes)
- Climate creates culture (the way we do things)
- A Culture sustained creates beliefs (the way man thinks)
- Beliefs create behavior (the way man acts)

The world's system is a counterculture of the Kingdom of God; and we, as Kingdom citizens, are called to contend for cultures. Today. in this fallen atmosphere, what is good is labeled as bad and bad is labeled good. For example, to be a virgin is bad and being promiscuous and homosexual is good. We are living in a confused society.

Now all 7-mountains (education, media, family, religion, entertainment, business, and government) are polluted atmospheres, filled with giants of lust, greed, and pride. Our assignment is to take out the giants by taking back atmospheres. Therefore, for every wicked presence there must be a prophetic response. When the Kingdom of God is missing, lower kingdoms rise up and pollute the atmosphere. Some examples include:

- Where there are no police – riots break out, thieves show up, and anarchy is present.
- Where there is no righteous government, demons pollute the offices.
- Where there are no fathers in authority, there will be insubordination and rebellion.

The time has come to invade atmospheres, within every sphere of society. The Spirit of God and the Kingdom of God is the highest dimension of authority. The Kingdom of God is the government of God, and the Spirit of God is the life of God. Both are necessary to shift atmospheres. We don't just cast out principalities and wicked ruling entities from the city, but we occupy our cities. We are called to deliver and set atmospheres free from their present condition and then transform the atmospheres with Heaven's culture.

The gospel of salvation is hygienic, it cleans people up, but the gospel the Kingdom will fill you up and transform atmospheres.

And he said unto them, It is not for you to know the times or the seasons, which the Father hath put in his own power. But ye shall receive power, after that the Holy Ghost is come upon you: and ye shall be witnesses unto me both in Jerusalem, and in all Judæa, and in Samaria, and unto the uttermost part of the earth. - Acts 1:7-8 KJV

There are three levels of authority: the Kingdom, a city, and a house. They come in that order, but the last will be first, and the first will be last. We must have authority at all three levels. You must have a strong house, then you're ready to influence and rule the city. Next, you'll rule in Christ's Kingdom. If we can't rule our house, we are not ready for the Kingdom, and we will be incapable to rule our cities.

...for if a man know not how to rule his own house, how shall he take care of the church of God? - 1 Timothy 3:5 KJV

As the Ekklesia we are called to make a prophetic impression on our cities and regions. The day of rhetoric is over, it's now time for reality. We must perform prophetic acts:

- If you see homeless people - we must build homes.
- If we see children sitting on the corners – we must build youth centers.
- If we see hungry people - we feed them and create jobs.
- If our educational systems are failing - we build schools.

Ye are of God, little children, and have overcome them: because greater is he that is in you, than he that is in the world. - 1 John 4:4 KJV

We must recover atmospheres. Note that the atmosphere does not control the Spirit, but the Spirit controls the atmosphere. This means that inferior environments are subject to your superior spirit! If we believe that, "greater is He that is in you," then you are not subject to anything outside of you. There are only 2 atmospheres in a city or sphere:

Sterile & Fertile – Cursed & Blessed – Wicked & Righteous - Evil & Good

We determine the atmosphere that we will live in. We take dominion by taking atmospheres.

And he that overcometh, and keepeth my works unto the end, to him will I give power over the nations. - Revelation 2:26 KJV

And he shewed me a pure river of water of life, clear as crystal, proceeding out of the throne of God and of the Lamb. In the midst of the street of it, and on either side of the river, was there the tree of life, which bare twelve manner of fruits, and yielded her fruit every month: and the leaves of the tree were for the healing of the nations. - Revelation 22:1-2 KJV

In this season, the Lord will raise up a Joseph Company that will heal the economy of cities and even nations. If the church is ever going to rule a nation, we must initially occupy key cities. For this to be fulfilled you must first have an apostolic ally-led, warring church established! This is filled with people who have the authority to cast down principalities and powers over that city. For example, New Castle is prophetically a key city here in Pennsylvania! Hell targets these key cities and harbors there through many different means such as: spirits of poverty, political corruption, drugs abuse, witchcraft, religious spirits, spirits of infirmity and the list goes on. This is a legal battle; therefore, it's won or lost in the courtroom of Heaven.

How Atmospheres Demonstrate the Kingdom of God

We are shifting seasons from proclaiming the Kingdom to DEMONSTRATING the Kingdom. From proclaiming to manifesting, we will see the Kingdom of God established on the Earth.

In the book of Daniel, Daniel and the 3 Hebrew boys changed the Babylonian atmosphere and culture by 5 ways:

- They created atmospheres.
- They had uncompromising beliefs.
- They had unshakable faith.
- They demonstrated the power of God.

- They planted the culture of Heaven upon the Earth.

Upper Room Encounters

Life is lived in levels. Before He ever performed miracles, Jesus created atmospheres. Atmospheres of honor, when created, invite miracles into our world. Upper room environments and atmospheres are important to our everyday life.

If the President of the United States, a mere man, can change the atmosphere because of his rank and order, he can force the change of environments and the shift of culture. How much more can we, as Kingdom citizens of the highest government in the universe, shift environments?

We are called to craft atmospheres. In the book of Acts chapter 2 the Upper Room influenced the Earth below. We are called to create Upper Room environments. These environments affect our homes, churches, businesses, and our cities. What takes place in the upper room determines everything underneath it. Elijah had an upper room and miracles resulted in his ministry. Who and What are over you determine your environment—good or bad.

Atmospheres are made up of ambience, culture, honor, climate, favor, presence, behavior, prayer, praise, excellence, and servant leadership. It's time to create and craft Upper Rooms. Grace, glory, and goodness flow out of Upper Room atmospheres and are channeled into every sphere of society. These Environments make us productive.

The Earth is dependent on what's in the Heavenlies. More specifically, we are reliant upon the Heavens. When we create Upper Room environments, we impose what's in

Heaven on the Earth. What took place in the upper room in Acts influenced everything and everyone below.

When Mary Magdalene broke open the alabaster box in worship, she altered the room. That act changed the atmosphere. The fragrance released an atmosphere of change and transformation (Luke 7:37-50). It takes sacrifice to create atmospheres. Mary sacrificed one year's salary when she poured out the perfume from that box. There is no such thing as a magic kingdom where this instantly happens. The one who serves at the table is greater than the one who sits at the table. We must learn to serve at times when we feel like it or not. Such sacrifices transform environments.

Chapter 8: Intercessory Teams

The church, at large, is boring and impotent. Furthermore, our present culture doesn't believe in us. We have 60-minute services and seeker friendly messages wrapped up in a pop culture church. When, in fact, God has called us to be an apostolic, prophetic culture church that equips, trains, and empowers the people of God. We should not strive to be popular, but prophetic. We are called to be a voice! We must respond to the call like Esther did. Mordecai warned her, "If you choose, not at this time to speak up, deliverance will come from elsewhere." Each and every one of us must respond to the call or miss the moment.

The true church of Jesus Christ attracts the world. When we emphasize virtue, truth, and Kingdom principles then, and only then, will we get Holy Ghost power. Christians need to quit conforming to the world. We must stop listening to the voices of Sanballat and Tobiah of our day. They only want to weaken the hands of Kingdom builders. Quit believing CNN and other fake news sources and start believing the good news of the gospel of the Kingdom of God.

And said unto them, It is written, My house shall be called the house of prayer; but ye have made it a den of thieves. - Matthew 21:13 KJV

The church of Jesus Christ must build a house a prayer to *all nations*. If we build it, they will come and see the goodness of God. Prayer is not designed for a small group of intercessors in a church. Jesus was talking to His emerging Ekklesia, when He said, "when you pray." Not if you pray, but when you pray. It would be absolutely impossible for my wife and I to have an intimate, covenant relationship without conversation. Likewise, your prayer life is a conversation with your Heavenly Father. Intercessory teams must be raised up to function by the spirit in the mantle of John the Baptist. By making the crooked places straight and the mountains plain, they will prepare the way for Apostolic-Prophetic influence in our regions.

In Acts 18, Apostle Paul took Aquila and Priscilla with him to Ephesus and left them there while he continued his journey. This husband-and-wife team of intercessors were planted there to soften the environment, to *shift the atmosphere*, and weaken the powers of darkness that ruled the city of Ephesus. They began to do the groundwork for Paul to return and take the city of Ephesus for the glory of God. When the Apostle Paul returned, the atmosphere was changed in Ephesus. There was a shift, and mighty signs and wonders resulted. The environment had changed so much that Paul was able to speak boldly and persuade men of "things concerning the Kingdom." Also, many were baptized in the Holy Ghost and disciples were made in Ephesus. Additionally, God did special miracles by the hands of the Apostle Paul (he shares that these were extraordinary, rare miracles).

I believe Ephesus had a sterile atmosphere until Aquila and Priscilla interceded. More than likely, this was the reason why Paul left and then returned. I truly believe that their intercessory prayer broke open the heavens over Ephesus. He waited until the atmosphere was right and ripe for ministry. After their prayers, the atmosphere was conducive to challenging demonic powers of sickness and witchcraft. The atmosphere was also ripe for a harvest. Acts 19:20 says, "So mightily grew the word of God and prevailed."

When we penetrate the spirit realm in intercession, we also change the earthly realm! Through intercessory prayer, we outrank the principalities and powers that oppose our cities' destinies. When we learn to pray from the heavenlies, we begin to see that the devil is not over us, but under us from our position in God. We were seated with Christ! This is the posture where we tread on serpents and scorpions. This is our position and our rank in God's Kingdom. You don't mess with God's Kingdom rank.

During this time in Ephesus, the Ephesians worshiped a false god named Diana. They built a temple in the city where the citizens would come and worship Diana. In 95 A.D. the emperor Domitian was assassinated, and John the apostle was released from prison on Patmos.
Immediately, he took an intercessory team with him, and went into the temple of Diana and addressed the spirit directly. He spoke a brief command to the spirit, and then the spirit fled. The high altar to Diana physically split into many pieces, like a bomb exploding. And 1/3 of the temple collapsed in ruins, as thought it was struck by an earthquake.

Polycarp, who was an eyewitness, wrote,

> "John entered the temple of Diana and stood before the high altar and commanded this principality to leave in the mighty name of Jesus saying, 'God of whose name every idol takes flight, and every demon and every unclean power, now let the demon that is here, take flight and thy name.' The building exploded, and the principality fled the city. Afterwards, the people cried out, 'There is but one God, the God of John! We are converted now that we have seen this marvelous works. Have mercy

upon us God, according to the will, and save us
from our great error!'"

All over the city, from the highest officials to the humblest
crowds, people came under deep conviction and pleaded
for God's mercy. The whole city was converted, and a new
cry went up. It was no longer towards Diana, the god of the
Ephesians, but the new cry was "Great is the God of John!"
In the coming days, we will see these kinds of
manifestations once again in our cities!

The Prayer of Agreement

Verily I say unto you, Whatsoever ye shall bind on earth
shall be bound in heaven: and whatsoever ye shall loose on
earth shall be loosed in heaven. Again I say unto you, That
if two of you shall agree on earth as touching any thing that
they shall ask, it shall be done for them of my Father which
is in heaven. For where two or three are gathered together
in my name, there am I in the midst of them. - Matthew
18:18-20 KJV

This verse doesn't say if you can get 2,000 people praying
for your city, then you may see some changes. You only
need two! The word *agree* translated from the Greek is the
English word for symphony. It literally means to make
exactly the same sound. The obvious and most natural
expression of this is a husband and wife praying together. If
you have this kind of prayer life, then you must have this
kind of symphonic harmony.

Husbands, in the same way be considerate as you live with
your wives, and treat them with respect as the weaker
partner and as heirs with you of the gracious gift of life, so
that nothing will hinder your prayers. - 1 Peter 3:7 NIV

Praying like this as a couple puts a wall of protection around your family. Church teams that flow together in real, symphonic harmony can put a protective wall around the members of the church so the devil cannot easily attack them. Agreeing in this manner not only forms an impregnable defense, but also becomes a very powerful weapon in the Kingdom.

Matthew 12:25 states, "every kingdom divided against itself is brought to desolation, and every city or house, divided against itself, will not stand." If there is true, symphonic unity, then it is impregnable, and can't be defeated. Attacks against us fail because we are a Kingdom. What would happen if we took these words seriously? First in our family, then our local church, and finally, for our whole city and region. A city divided against itself cannot stand. Do you know of any city in the world where all the Christians are in symphonic harmony? Can you imagine what would happen if they were in real symphony? The early church did. They were a community, living in common unity. They turned that known world upside down!

They could ask anything they wanted, and it would be done for them. They could bind anything, and it would be bound. They could loose anything and it would be loosed. This symphonic spiritual harmony equates to authority. There's tremendous power in real symphonic harmony, and there is a tremendous weakness in division. Choose well.

Aggressive Agreement

Aggressive agreement is more powerful than any individual faith. The power of agreement is the greatest faith because it's corporate faith. Therefore, our corporate faith is greater than any individual faith.

Peter therefore was kept in prison: but prayer was made without ceasing of the church unto God for him. - Acts 12:5 KJV

We see in this passage, the principal of aggressive agreement. Peter was in prison and the church corporately begin to pray for him. As a result, an angel of the Lord delivered him, and he immediately went to Rhoda's house, where they were all praying for him, to share the good news. When he arrived, the church did not believe that it was Peter. It seemed as if they were praying for Peter but did not have faith that he would be delivered. This story reveals the power of aggressive agreement. Many did not have the faith for Peter's deliverance, but because of aggressive agreement, Heaven answered their prayer.

Prayer Points

Keys to releasing Kingdom prayers into the Earth:

1. Pray with the heart of Jesus.
2. Pray out the revelation that the Holy Ghost gives you - prophetic prayers.
3. Pray in the corporate anointing - the church must pray corporately as we are called to judge the world and we judge it by calling it back to Christ.
4. Pray imprecatory prayers - prayers against spiritual wickedness and against rulers of darkness. The Psalms are full of these imprecatory prayers. We must learn how to pray against evil (e.g. praying these prayers against psychic centers and a radical terrorist group in my city forced them to pack up and leave).

5. Pray from the heavenlies - pray the answer not the problem.
6. Pray with authority - praying from our position, seated in Christ.
7. Pray in aggressive agreement - corporate aggressive agreement is greater than any man's individual faith.

Characteristics of an Authentic Warring Church

- Powerful corporate prayer life
- Governmental praise and worship
- Manifesting signs, wonders, and healings
- Living the ascended life
- Great grace and favor upon the whole church
- Not one feeble or weak among the saints
- No needy people among the ranks
- Preaching the Kingdom of God
- Healing the sick
- Casting out demons
- A prophetic company of believers
- Sending the saints to infiltrate society
- Influencing all 7 spheres of society

The Heavens Rule

*And whereas they commanded to leave the stump of the tree roots; thy kingdom shall be sure unto thee, after that thou shalt have known that **THE HEAVENS DO RULE**.* - Daniel 4:26 KJV

The way we rule the world is to rule the heavens. We know that the prince and power of the air (satan) rules from the second heaven. Once we occupy the heavenly realm, we can easily rule the city. Picketing, marches, and campaigns have little effect. By first binding the strongman in the heavens, we can then plunder his house and rule the territory. Once we gain the realm of the spirit, we can influence the natural realm.

Penetrating and occupying the heavens is our present assignment. But it will take aggressive faith and persevering prayer. Once we possess the realm of the heavenlies, then we can enforce the Kingdom of God, the rule and reign of God in the realm of the earth. Praying out of the finished work of the cross is true Kingdom prayer! Matt Stafford, the quarterback for the LA Rams said, "I play from a place of victory." Is that not what we are called to do? We don't fight for the victory; we fight from the victory! We are called to enforce the finished work of Calvary.

Planting the Heavens in the Earth

Thy kingdom come. Thy will be done in earth, as it is in heaven. - Matthew 6:10 KJV

And I have put my words in thy mouth, and I have covered thee in the shadow of mine hand, that I may plant the heavens, and lay the foundations of the earth, and say unto Zion, Thou art my people. - Isaiah 51:16 KJV

The Bible is a window to all that is in the heavenly realm. When the Holy Spirit breathes on the Word of God, that inspired NOW WORD is yours to plant in the Earth.

We know there is no sickness in Heaven only health; therefore, we can plant health in the Earth God may give you words of knowledge to accomplish this. We know that Heaven is filled with joy, full of righteousness, peace, love, mercy, forgiveness, and many blessings. Therefore, let's plant it in the earth.

Planting the heavens in the Earth begins with prophetic intercession, that sees and births the will of God into the planet! What you want to see for your city in the spirit— you must plant it! So many believers expect instantaneous miracles to occur all the time. However, Jesus spent quality time sharing parables about the process of sowing and reaping. There have been prophetic words sown as seeds decades ago into our ministry here in New Castle that are just now coming to pass. With faith and patience, we receive the promises of God. Every seed goes through a process.

You and I are Kingdom farmers. We're called to be fruitful, so get busy sowing seeds. Sow seeds into people's lives, sow seeds into your ministry, sow seeds in your family, your children, your marriage, and sow seeds into your city. Many expect a harvest without sowing any seed. Do you know why my future is so bright? Because I planted the Heavens in my personal field, and in other's fields.

"Whatever man sows that will he reap." Are you seed-minded, or need-minded? Your seed never reveals the past; it reveals your future. Every day is an opportunity to sow seeds so don't miss the opportunity. Universities are no longer sowing seeds of knowledge into the students; instead, they are sowing seeds that are indoctrinating the students with their Woke agenda and their vain philosophies. Their culture contradicts the Word of the Lord and His Kingdom culture.

Then Jesus sent the multitude away, and went into the house: and his disciples came unto him, saying,

*Declare unto us the parable of the tares of the field.
He answered and said unto them, He that soweth
the good seed is the Son of man; the enemy that
sowed them is the devil; the harvest is the end of the
world; and the reapers are the angels. As therefore
the tares are gathered and burned in the fire; so
shall it be in the end of this world. The Son of man
shall send forth his angels, and they shall gather out
of his kingdom all things that offend, and them
which do iniquity; and shall cast them into a
furnace of fire: there shall be wailing and gnashing
of teeth. Then shall the righteous shine forth as the
sun in the kingdom of their Father. Who hath ears
to hear, let him hear.* - Matthew 13:36-37, 39-43
KJV

Jesus tells us that the tares and the wheat have been sown
into the same field and will grow together, but we are
promised at the end of the age He will gather out from His
Kingdom all the things that offend and those that do
iniquity. God's Kingdom will prevail!

Prayer Strategies

Keys to serve and transform a city:

- Prophesy and pray out the city of the future.
- Stand against strategies that divide the city.
- Change the landscape of the city by praying from
  the Heavenlies.
- Make decrees that close evil gates.
- Breathe new life into old things.
- Pull provision out of the Heavens attracting
  resources (e.g. planting the Heavens by your
  words).

- Take authority over opposing things by releasing the opposite (overcome evil with good).
- Raise up and release Daniels and Josephs.
- Solve the problems in our city.
- Release prophetic prayer seeds into barren structures.
- Create a legacy of the sustainable Presence of God for our children (changing culture).
- Create Kingdom businesses and enterprises that transform city economics and influence the atmosphere.

Keys to warring for cities & nations:

- We battle in the spirit before boots on the ground (air-assault before ground troops).
- Only through persistent prayer will this occur and then signs and wonders will manifest (once this occurs cities become war zones).
- The strongman must be bound in the Heavens before you spoil his house (plunder your city and nation for a harvest of souls and wealth transfer).

But if I cast out devils by the Spirit of God, then the kingdom of God is come unto you. Or else how can one enter into a strong man's house, and spoil his goods, except he first bind the strong man? and then he will spoil his house. - Matthew 12:28-29 KJV

To transform a city, it will take travailing, prophetic intercession until the dream is birthed.

Ask, and it shall be given you; seek, and ye shall find; knock, and it shall be opened unto you.
-        Matthew   7:7   KJV

Chapter 9: An Apostolic & Prophetic Culture

Apostolic and Prophetic Teams

We must gather the apostles and prophets to work congruently, and as they do their marriage will give birth to the promises made over our cities. Together we will disciple men and women to take territory, influence our present society, and transform culture with Christ's Kingdom.

If we are going to apostolically advance the Kingdom in our cities, we will need prophetic processes and protocols. Apostles and apostolic teams employ military strategies to attract the prophets. Together, they disciple cities and nations, take territory and change culture.

To take the city, we must create a prophetic culture. Being prophetic is knowing the desire of God—His passions, interests, and purposes. Harnessing this type of culture demands that we prophetically speak the mind of Christ into our cities and the lives of the citizens.

Sadly, most prophets are so undeveloped they can't compete with cults in the marketplace. The voice of the occult (the serpent) redirected Adam and Eve into sin. So, God spoke as a prophet to reestablish his purposes in the earth. Mankind is continually led by the voice of a serpent, and not God. But God is raising up a new breed of prophets in the Earth to redirect, redefine, and restore the Lord's true identity for His people, cities, and the nations.

In this past season we've had many abuses and we hosted disorderly prophets in the church. All New Testament prophecy must be tested. Many prophets on Facebook and social media are illegitimate, cyber prophets. True prophets work with prophetic teams and work under the order of apostolic oversight. In the New Testament, prophets always functioned in partnership with apostles. The prophetic is about to be amplified. We are migrating into a new realm of the prophetic. It's time to champion and mature the prophetic.

What makes the prophetic weak and weird?

1. Not being connected to apostolic grace.
2. Living in a silo structure independently.

Prophetic Protocol

- NEVER CLAIM PROPHETIC INFALLIBILITY
- NEVER PUT DATES ON ANY PROPHECY
- DO NOT POLLUTE THE PROPHETIC WELL WITH CONSPIRACIES
- DO NOT ACTIVATE UNTIL YOU'RE TRAINED
- LOYALTY AND ALLEGIANCE TO ANOTHER CAN CAUSE YOU TO PROPHESY INACCURATELY
- POLITICAL ALLEGIANCE CAN INFLUENCE PROPHECY
- DO NOT PROPHESY ELECTION PROPHECIES
- NEVER ATTACK PROPHETS WHO MISSED IT, BUT INVESTIGATE THE REASONS WHY THEIR WORD DID NOT COME TO PASS

Prophets and Politics

Where in the Bible do you find the words: politics, politician, or political? As the religious spirit is an imposter, so is the political spirit. The political spirit masquerades in the place of God's government.

Politics has nothing to do with God's Kingdom. It is not used in scripture once. When we get engaged with the political spirit, it's like being engaged to the religious spirit. Jesus warned us to stay away from the scribes and Pharisees. The scribes represent the political spirit, while the Pharisees represent the religious spirit.

Politics is not God's government, and it's not part of His rule. May I give you a warning, stay free from the political spirit for it has destroyed many men and women in ministry. What the religious spirit has done to the church, so will the political spirit do as well. Do not get tangled up in that political spirit.

Politics relates to the soul while the Kingdom relates to the spirit. Politics will shipwreck leadership. You never hear me discuss politics in the pulpit. We are part of a government that's higher. I'm not telling you to not vote, but please don't vote Democrat or Republican. Vote Kingdom. Vote for whoever's policies best reflect the Kingdom of Heaven. I've watched several prophetic voices on Facebook lose their edge after they become extremely engaged in politics.

In the Old and New Testaments, we see apostles and prophets speaking to kings and pharaohs, but they only did so by the unction of the Holy Spirit.

The prophetic is very simple: it is reconnecting people to the voice of our Heavenly Father.

Prophetic Words Over Cities

It's important that we know prophetically the words that God has spoken over our cities and states. Here are examples of prophetic words spoken over my state of Pennsylvania.

- It was prophesied by Apostle Dennis Wiedrick that "as Levi was in the loins of Abraham, likewise all 49 states are in the lions of Pennsylvania." And we must, "now call forth the apostles in our state."

- Dr. William Hinn prophesied a confirming word that "The 49 states are in the womb of Pennsylvania."

- Prophet Alan Vincent prophesied over Pennsylvania and said, "Pennsylvania is nearer to a move of God than any part of the US. PA is a mighty, devil-crushing church. PA could be the start of a mighty move of God, spreading across the nation and touching nations. People will jump on planes to come to PA and see what God is doing. It could be an Azusa Street 1,000 times more."

- Clay Nash prophesied, "Pennsylvania is in a key position to trigger things; there is an Authority and Anointing coming out of Pennsylvania now!" He went on to say that "we hold the key, and we must pick up the torch of William Penn." He stated that, "Pennsylvania will deal with nations."

It's important that you declare the prophetic words spoken over your city and states. Proclaim them over and over until they begin to manifest.

This charge I commit unto thee, son Timothy, according to the prophecies which went before on thee, that thou by them mightest war a good warfare.... - 1 Timothy 1:18 KJV

Defining Apostles and Apostolic Resource Centers

Apostles and apostolic churches deliver regions from demonic technology (demonic, principalities, and cultural principles that rule the city) and establish Kingdom culture in their sphere. In this cultural war, our calling is to establish Heaven's Kingdom culture.

Apostolic churches are governmental branches of Heaven upon the earth. These apostolic centers are filled with Kingdom ambassadors representing the Kingdom of heaven upon the earth. Their assignment is to colonize the earth with God's Kingdom culture. We are on an apostolic mission. Apostles in biblical times were admirals sent by the king with a trained apostolic military might. This military might consists of trained, disciplined, committed, loyal, equipped, and mature covenant people.

In apostolic centers, the apostles validate the life, anointing, grace, assignments and callings in men and women (not their gifts and talents). Apostles and apostolic teams revive things, restore things, renew things, resurrect things, remove things, reform things, refresh things and release things. Apostles prepare apostolic teams for warfare and to occupy territory, equipped with strategies for various kinds of warfare. The primary grace upon apostles is to father sons and form CHRIST in the sons of God. Apostles give sons a place of inheritance.

Apostolic churches build things that last, crafting a work that outlives them. Apostles and apostolic teams lead the future. With no respect for man's opinions, they only esteem what the WORD says. Apostles generate unity that is based on the Word. We are segregated in the body of Christ because of not knowing truth. How can two walk together except they agree? Apostolic churches are marked for increase. This will include additions of people, favor, glory, healings, miracles, wisdom, revelation, wealth, and influence.

Earmarks Of Apostolic Centers

1. Manifestations of the Lord's Presence (healings, miracles)
2. Governmental praise and worship (celebration)
3. Citywide impact (influencing and occupying the 7 mountains)
4. House of prayer to all nations (multiracial church community)
5. New wine (divine expressions of joy)
6. Sent saints (destroying the works of the enemy)
7. Sons and daughters (Kingdom succession and legacy)
8. Vision (prophetic insight and foresight)
9. Covering (spiritual fathers and mothers)
10. Spirit of excellence (serving in a meritorious way)
11. Spirit of honor (high levels of respect)
12. Hand of God (fivefold ministry)
13. Corporate anointing (Body of Christ ministry)
14. Discipleship (schools of ministry)
15. Succession plan (empowering our seed)
16. Name of the Lord is in the House of the Lord (fruit of the Spirit)
17. Prophecy (prophetic words from the Lord)
18. Servanthood (serving the needs of the city)
19. Apostles' doctrine (accurate teaching and preaching)

20. Evangelism (harvest of souls)
21. Wealth building (Kingdom resources)
22. Kingdom prayer (intercessors)
23. City outreaches (food distributions, reformation strategies)

Apostolic Warfare and Kingdom Government

Apostolic warfare is released through praise/worship, prayer, decrees, prophetic acts, wealth creation and evangelism. These work together to eliminate demonic tyranny (unrestrained exercise of power) bringing down demonic forces.

Devils will come down, not because of a prayer or rebuke alone, but because a government is in place. The government backs the decrees, (devils only obey rank). Apostolic government centers drive out demonic predators. They don't respond to guerrilla warfare that is impromptu, unprepared, and unorganized combat.

Jesus warned us to beware of these two spirits:
- The leaven of Herod – political spirits
- The leaven of the Pharisees – religious spirits

And he charged them, saying, Take heed, beware of the leaven of the Pharisees, and of the leaven of Herod. - Mark 8:15 KJV

The Kingdom of God is a government. As ambassadors of Christ's Kingdom, we have spiritual immunity. Devils harass religions but they cannot harass a government established by an apostolic and prophetic culture.

Chapter 10: It's Time to Build

Presently, we are in a "building season." This season will unfold with the following types of leadership characteristics:

Engineering Leaders: The Lord is presently raising up these leaders to build. Architectural leaders are only concerned with beauty or appearance; they will be irrelevant in this new season. Instead, the true Kingdom engineers create the right structures and correct the alignment of each project. The function of engineering leaders reveals how we must realign to be essential in this present hour.

Wise-master Builders: These times demand for us to be able to define what we are building. First and foremost, we are building people - a certain kind of people who are mantled with the anointing of the sons of Issachar. They "understood the times and knew what Israel ought to do!" This combination creates prophetic and apostolic people. "Understanding the times" is the prophetic edge and "knowing what to do" is the apostolic edge. Prophetically, we scan the Heavens to hear and see what God is doing! Apostolically, we employ strategies to establish the culture of Heaven upon the earth.

And of the children of Issachar, which were men that had understanding of the times, to know what Israel ought to do; the heads of them were two hundred; and all their brethren were at their commandment. - 1 Chronicles 12:32 KJV

A Corporate Expression: We will learn to operate in companies in this building season. The days of silo ministries are over. This is the time for the corporate anointing. We know that one will put a 1,000 to flight but two will put 10,000 to flight.

Thus saith the LORD, As the new wine is found in the cluster, and one saith, Destroy it not; for a blessing is in it: so will I do for my servants' sakes, that I may not destroy them all. - Isaiah 65:8 KJV

Prophetic People: We must choose to be prophetic, not popular, in this season. By choosing the prophetic, we will not attract everyone, but we will attract builders.

And Moses said unto him, Enviest thou for my sake? would God that all the LORD's people were prophets, and that the LORD would put his spirit upon them! - Numbers 11:29 KJV

Unselfish Hearts: This is a season to put aside selfish desires. By laying down our own egos and ideas, we can pursue His perfect design to build. God is looking for a generation that "loves not their lives even unto the death."

And they overcame him by the blood of the Lamb, and by the word of their testimony; and they loved not their lives unto the death. - Revelation 12:11 KJV

Divine Urgency: There is no altar call to inaugurate builders; builders never need to be coerced to build—it's just in them to do it! Instead of just talking about the vision, Kingdom builders just build it NOW. Why? Because the blueprint is within us. Once you dream, you must build.

Visionary Leaders: The prophet said, "Without vision, the people perish." Therefore, with vision we will prosper. At the core of this leadership is the power of vision. Vision is the powerful force that makes a dream a reality. A godly vision will drive every decision within the community! Vision, a dynamic force, empowers men and women to fulfill destiny.

Therefore, we are putting a new face on the church. We must build accurately according to the Word of the Lord using principles and patterns from scripture. There are two kinds of people in the church today: there are blessers and there are builders. Those who want the blessing and those who want to build. Builders do not need to be told to build; it's intrinsic to their nature. They need to know you are offering them a place to serve and fulfill their calling in God. Find the builders and let's build together!

God's Order for Building and Planting

Then the LORD put forth his hand, and touched my mouth. And the LORD said unto me, Behold, I have put my words in thy mouth. See, I have this day set thee over the nations and over the kingdoms, to root out, and to pull down, and to destroy, and to throw down, to build, and to plant. - Jeremiah 1:9-10 KJV

Then said he, Lo, I come to do thy will, O God. He taketh away the first, that he may establish the second. - Hebrews 10:9 KJV

It's time to build and plant. Rooting up, pulling down, destroying, and throwing down all precede this work of building and planting! Removing the first to establish the second is God's divine order. The Lord intentionally disrupts a city in preparation for building apostolically. The Kingdom of God is disruptive. If you're afraid of not being liked, you're sitting at the wrong table. Jesus told His disciples "If the world hates you; you know that it hated Me before you." We are called to be a voice of influence.

First is the work of prophetic ministry; the second is the work of apostolic ministry. Many times, in preparation to transform our city, we see God uprooting and pulling down things. This should not discourage us. It's God preparing the landscape for us to build and plant His Kingdom in our cities. Where there is an apostle there are builders. Apostles are wise master-builders.

According to the grace of God which is given unto me, as a wise masterbuilder, I have laid the foundation, and another buildeth thereon. But let every man take heed how he buildeth thereupon. - 1 Corinthians 3:10 KJV

A Nehemiah and Ezra anointing is in this present season, but it can only be utilized in your life if you rise up and build. The blessing comes when we build and when we build God will bless. Builders will be given toolboxes. In these toolboxes are a variety of tools: the gifts of the Holy Ghost (spiritual tools), wealth, valuable relationships, and a variance of resources. Connections will become tools that create Kingdom synergy for building. But these toolboxes will only be given to those who are building the corporate Kingdom vision for cities and nations.

One of the things we must build is a house of prayer for all nations. Daniel exemplifies this principle and pattern. Daniel changed the political map through prayerful devotion, praying Cyrus into office. Strategic prophetic words that have been declared can also become our motivation for prayer.

After this manner therefore pray ye: Our Father which art in heaven, Hallowed be thy name. Thy kingdom come. Thy

will be done in earth, as it is in heaven. And lead us not into temptation, but deliver us from evil: For thine is the kingdom, and the power, and the glory, for ever. Amen. - Matthew 6:9-10, 13 KJV

Superimposition praying is essential for advancing the Kingdom. Superimposition prayers release:
- THE KINGDOM (divine government)
- THE POWER (divine authority)
- AND THE GLORY (divine presence)

In this season, **we pray the answer!**

Chapter 11: The Ekklesia: A Treatise on the 21st Century Church

Jesus told His disciples, "Upon this rock I'll **BUILD** my **EKKLESIA** and the gates of hell shall not prevail against it" [emphasis added].

He was explaining that when hell has invaded an area, you have the keys of the Kingdom of Heaven to overpower it and to influence that same place with His Kingdom power and authority.

The Kingdom of God is a system in God. The kingdoms of this world system will become the systems of our God. The Ekklesia is a Sending Company; we send men and women into the systems of this world. When they go as salt and light, they infiltrate and influence that sphere.

Zacchaeus was a chief publican and very wealthy. Once he encountered Christ, he said he would give half of his goods to the poor and give a fourfold return of all that he had stolen. Consider what might've happened when Zacchaeus went back to work the next day! He was the chief overseer in the system he operated; now he was commissioned by an encounter with Jesus and would shift the system. Now the system would come under his influence and anointing.

And Zacchæus stood, and said unto the Lord; Behold, Lord, the half of my goods I give to the poor; and if I have taken any thing from any man by false accusation, I restore him fourfold. And Jesus said unto him, This day is salvation come to this house, forsomuch as he also is a son of Abraham. - Luke 19:8-9 KJV

We are called to be "SYSTEM SHIFTERS" and by getting enough people full of the Holy Ghost who are empowered and equipped to go into the city and influence it, the whole city can come under Kingdom influence.

We see this principle with the woman at the well in Samaria. Jesus "read her mail" by giving her a word of knowledge. She left the encounter and ran back to her city and brought the whole city to the well to meet Jesus. She influenced her whole city because of one encounter. We are to lead people into an encounter with Jesus, then commission them.

The woman then left her waterpot, and went her way into the city, and saith to the men, Come, see a man, which told me all things that ever I did: is not this the Christ? Then they went out of the city, and came unto him. - John 4:28-30 KJV

Every church must become a Kingdom university. In America, the SAT scores among students are the lowest in the world. This downward spiral began in the early 1960's when prayer was banned from schools. The baby boomer generation of believers fell asleep in the 60's and 70's losing many spiritual battles, like Roe versus Wade, the renown Supreme court case.

The General Assembly

But ye are come unto mount Sion, and unto the city of the living God, the heavenly Jerusalem, and to an innumerable company of angels, To the general assembly and church of the firstborn, which are written in heaven, and to God the Judge of all, and to the spirits of just men made perfect. - Hebrews 12:22-23

The Lord calls us His General Assembly. As the church, we gather as the General Assembly and pass legislation.

Through the release of Heaven's decrees, we address social, governmental and community issues. The church stands as the governing body of the Kingdom of Heaven on Earth. Jesus, King of kings and Lord of lords, is the head over His Body of lords, who unite as His General Assembly.

In the Greek the word lord has multiple meanings that include: one who has power to decide, the possessor of a thing, one who has control, a governor, a person possessing supreme authority, a controller, and a respectful title of a master or sir.

While this brief treatise is certainly not intended to be a "know it all" or exclusive coverage of this imperative topic, it is nonetheless intended as a catalytic primer for the gathering of apostles, prophets, evangelists, pastors, teachers, entrepreneurs, and other men and women in the ranks of God's Kingdom to join together as the General Assembly of the Lord Jesus Christ.

The challenge is clear: destiny is in the hands of the church. Therefore, the church of Jesus Christ has no alternative but to respond to this call and it is indeed an ordination for such a time as this.

Not forsaking the assembling of ourselves together as the manner of some do, but exhorting one another and so much more as we see the day approaching. - Hebrews 10:25

I do not believe that the writer of the book of Hebrews was only speaking of the gathering together of the Hebrew church, but the assembling together as the General Assembly in Hebrews chapter 12. The church is the governing body of the Kingdom of Heaven on the Earth.

In past and current political examples, Great Britain upholds a House of Lords, and the United States of America maintains two houses, the House of Representatives, and the Senate. In Scripture, Jesus called the church to be "a house of prayer to all nations." The word house means a body of lords united in their legislative capacity. In God's economy His house is the estate of a Kingdom, assembled as the legislative body. The early church operated in the highest court of God's Kingdom on the earth (we are seated with Christ in heavenly places).

Ekklesia means parliament is in session; it's a general assembly of lords. We are the house of the Lord. The Lord said that we are house of prayer to all nations. The word house means; a body of lords, united in their legislative capacity. Being a house of prayer does not just mean a people who come together and pray for each other's needs. It means so much more. As a house of prayer, we are a body of lords, coming together through prayer, prophetic proclamations, and apostolic decrees. We do Kingdom business in the spirit and pass righteous judgments over our community.

The church of Jesus Christ has been commissioned by Heaven to govern the territory where they have been assigned. The Ekklesia of Jesus Christ is a Parliament in session operating as the General Assembly of lords who decree righteous judgments and pass legislation collectively in the sphere of their domain.

The early church in the book of Acts operated as the highest court in God's Kingdom on the Earth. Simply put, the church is the governing body of the Kingdom of Heaven upon the Earth.

The destiny of our cities, states, and nation, depend on the prayers and decrees of the church. The church is called to come together in prayer and declare the will and mind of God over our cities, states, and nation.

I tell you the truth, whatever you forbid on earth will be forbidden in heaven and whatever you permit on earth will be permitted in heaven. - Matthew 18:18 NLT

With the keys of the Kingdom, we have been given the authority to bind and to loose. These are legal terms. Therefore, what we permit shall be permitted and what we don't permit will not be permitted, this reveals the true authority of the church. We experienced this in New Castle, PA when we passed legislation and released restraining orders against a radical Muslim group that tried to take over our city and three psychic centers that strategically set up camp in our city, and several drug rings in our city. Within several months of passing legislation, and releasing restraining orders, these groups fled our city for the glory of God!

We must not permit sickness, poverty, witchcraft, prostitution, drug lording, crime, abortion, pornography, or any unrighteousness to reside in our cities, states, and nation. Rising with the keys of the Kingdom in hand, we must execute judgment against the powers of darkness.

When Jesus gave His apostles the keys to the Kingdom of Heaven, He took His apostles to the darkest place on earth (Caesarea Phillipi) and said, "I give you legal authority to open the Heavens and shut down hell." When we gather together as the Lord's General Assembly, we pray, "God's Kingdom come and His will be done in earth as it is in Heaven". Therefore, we exercise our covenant rights and authority as kings to bring God's Kingdom into full manifestation in the earth.

Now then we are ambassadors for Christ, as though God did beseech you by us: we pray you in Christ's stead, be ye reconciled to God. - 2 Corinthians 5:20

We are sent here as ambassadors of Christ, representing the Kingdom of Heaven upon the earth. As ambassadors we've been given spiritual immunity in the spheres where God has assigned us. The church is not to separate itself from the world but to invade it and change it.

Behold, I give unto you power to tread on serpents and scorpions, and over all the power of the enemy: and nothing shall by any means hurt you. Notwithstanding in this rejoice not, that the spirits are subject unto you; but rather rejoice, because your names are written in heaven. - Luke 10:19-20 KJV

Jesus said, "Occupy till I come." He also prayed to His Heavenly Father, "I pray you take them not out of the world but keep them from evil." This is the true church that Jesus Christ is raising up in the present hour. She is a military might, invading every sphere of society, and filling it with the glory of God.

For the earth shall be filled with the knowledge of the glory of the LORD, as the waters cover the sea. - Habakkuk 2:14 KJV

And he hath on his vesture and on his thigh a name written, KING of kings, and LORD of lords.
- Revelation 19:16 KJV

As the King, Jesus reproduces kings, and as the Lord He reproduces lords. All lords have a domain and land that they manage. It's where we get the term landlords. It's time for the church to move into lordship! We are being commissioned to govern the land, and to possess it. Interestingly, during the time I was receiving this revelation, I received the right to assume the honorific title of Lord Mark Edward Kauffman and my wife, Lady Jill Ann Kauffman under the laws of England. This was a prophetic sign to my wife and me that it was time for the church to begin to move into its lordship responsibilities and authority.

The church was never meant to be a subculture amid the world around us. We are designed to be a Kingdom culture that not only opposes the existing culture but radically changes it. Many have called the church a counterculture. The church is not a counterculture; we are *the only* culture that God had purposed for the planet.

As an apostolic church here in New Castle, Pennsylvania, Jubilee Ministries International, is an embassy, representing God's government. We must stop thinking of our local churches as a religious edifice. They are government agencies. We gather together as key Kingdom influencers. As we gather as the Ekklesia of Jesus Christ, we conduct government business. Our government (the Kingdom of God) owns the planet. "The Earth is the Lord's and the fullness thereof and all they that dwell therein." Governments are trying to run a planet that's not theirs. It belongs to the Lord Jesus Christ and His church. Jesus told us that the meek, shall inherit the Earth. Jesus has already bound the strongman; now we must reclaim the planet for King Jesus! We must make Jesus the King of every sphere of society. We currently have a mandate to transform our cities for the glory of God in our lifetime.

The Kingdom's Governmental Arm

O sing unto the Lord a new song; for he hath done marvelous things: his right hand, and his holy arm, hath gotten him the victory. - Psalm 98:1

Jesus is King of kings and Lord of lords. The church, as kings and lords of His Kingdom, is the governmental arm of Heaven, charged to proclaim, impart, and demonstrate the Kingdom of God in the Earth. As we can now see, the church does much more than pour oil into the wounds of the saints, encourage one another, and fellowship together (though these experiences are necessary). We are the Ekklesia, a military might, sent by God to transform society. The church is called to be a governmental branch of Heaven upon the earth and colonize the earth, with Heaven's realities! Invading every sphere of society as salt and light, we influence it and transform it to look like Heaven. Every local church must become a Kingdom embassy, a governmental branch of Heaven upon the earth. Every church must become a Kingdom University, training and teaching its members.

- *The right hand of the Lord is exalted: the right hand of the Lord does valiantly.* – Psalm 118:16

- *Behold, the Lord GOD will come with strong hand, and his arm shall rule for him: behold, his reward is with him, and his work before him.* - Isaiah 40:10 KJV

- *Awake, awake, put on strength, O arm of the LORD; awake, as in the ancient days, in the generations of old. Art thou not it that hath cut Rahab, and wounded the dragon?* - Isaiah 51:9 KJV

- *The LORD hath made bare his holy arm in the eyes of all the nations; and all the ends of the earth shall see the salvation of our God.* - Isaiah 52:10 KJV

Jesus is the VINE, and we are His branches! As we can see in the above passages, the arm or branch of God is an extension of the Lord's rule and reign in the Earth. To rule with Christ is our position in Christ; to reign with Christ is our execution of that rule.

Reigning in Life as Kings

For if by one man's offense death reigned by one; much more they which receive abundance of grace and of the gift of righteousness shall reign in life by one, Jesus Christ. - Romans 5:17

Fivefold leaders are called to equip, impact, empower, prepare, and charge the saints to change the world to look like Heaven. The Kingdom church is not a building where we meet as a maintenance center to solely maintain our salvation until Jesus comes, but it's an empowerment center to train the saints to reign in this life as kings (see my book, *Kings Arise*).

This season is the season of dominion! A season of kingship. We are ushering in the kingship of all believers. As kings we have dominion because the King of kings lives in us and is seated in us right now, and we are seated with Him in heavenly places. We are facing a counterculture dominion in the world that is opposing the God's Kingdom dominion. The world's dominion is like Saul who wants to destroy every emerging David. The worldly dominion rapes the sons of God of their dominion. It's like Laban, who wants to suppress you of your purpose and uses your favor

89

for his purposes. The dominion of the world is like Nebuchadnezzar who wants to burn up your future. Like Pharaoh, this world's dominion wants to destroy our children by making them slaves to its system. The dominion of the world is like Herod who wants to abort our seed from coming forth from the womb. The dominion of the world is like Adoni-Bezek, who hates the apostolic. In the Old Testament, he cut off the big toes and thumbs of those who opposed him. Hating the apostolic so badly, he will use everything in his power to cut it off in order to make the church lame so it cannot run into its destiny. The dominion of the world is like King Darius who will place you in a lion's den, full of people who hate you and constantly oppose the Christ that is within you.

Presently, there is an urgency by the Spirit of the Living God for the Ekklesia to assemble as a military might of kings to influence, impact, transform, and take dominion over the world. **Reclaiming cities prophetically is our current call**. Apostolic and Prophetic people have an anointing on them to scan the Heavens and discern the spirit realm. They pull down strongholds ruling over their cities.

And hast made us unto our God kings and priests: and we shall reign on the earth. - Revelation 5:10 KJV

As KINGS we dislodge principalities and powers over the region, drive out demonic powers, repossess land, create wealth, and win souls. As PRIESTS we are to bless and prophecy over everything and everyone in our sphere. We not only pray, but declare strong decrees to enforce, "THY KINGDOM COME!" As priests we pray thy Kingdom come, but as kings we enforce that Kingdom.

If my people, which are called by my name, shall humble themselves, and pray, and seek my face, and turn from their wicked ways; then will I hear from heaven, and will forgive their sin, and will heal their land. - 2 Chronicles 7:14 KJV

We pray looking over our cities and not from under the Heavens but seated in heavenly places. We are looking from Heaven's perspective! There is no poverty in heaven, no homelessness, no hunger, no sickness, no diseases, no witchcraft, no drug abuse, no AIDS, no perversion, no murder, no rape, no abortion, no fatherless, no COVID-19, and no sin in the Heavens. The Lord wants to heal the land, reaching the non-productive areas of our cities.

Thy kingdom come. Thy will be done in earth, as it is in heaven. - Matthew 6:10 KJV

Principalities and powers are on assignment, they have rank and order, but so do we. We are a military-might in Christ's Kingdom. Together we outrank all our enemies. We are here to disrupt and displace the powers of darkness with CHRIST'S KINGDOM of righteousness, peace, and joy! If you're not in rank and order, you have no rank and authority over principalities and powers.

One man can chase away 1,000 of my people! Two men can chase away 10,000 of them! - Deuteronomy 32:30 EASY

If two of you, only two! Group prayer can change world events. Ten out of 100,000 people rule over 5 main systems: media, education, finance, religion, and politics! The exponential power of the corporate anointing makes us dangerous! One puts 1,000 to flight while 2 can chase 10,000.

Ch 12: Go into All the World: The 7 Mountain Mandate

When Israel crossed over the Jordan into the Promised Land, there were 7 nations in Canaan that they were called to occupy. These 7 nations symbolize the 7 mountains of influence in our culture today: religion, family, sports/entertainment, education, government, media, and business. Like Caleb of the Promised Land, a new breed of "Calebs" are being mantled to remove giants and seize their mountains. It's time for the church to become essential to our culture.

What are the giants of this day? First and foremost, it is a season of warfare over communication. The media mountain and educational mountain are controlling the minds of men and women. We must recapture these two mountains from the start with authentic prophetic voices to control them. Our K-12 schools and universities must become prophetic schools. The current systems are indoctrinating our children with woke ideologies. Parents, please do everything you can to get your children out of American schools. Education has ceased while indoctrination has taken over. The National Education Association said their causes are to support LGBTQ, to support abortion for students, and to support gun control. This has nothing to do with students being educated or the role teachers should have in education. Parents, sacrifice now or pay later.

These kinds of teachers and professors think they're gods. Much like the serpent who deceived Eve, they determine what's good or evil. If you don't agree with them, they will fight you and come after you. Sexualizing kids in school is not the teacher's job; they no longer teach things that matter. Now students have to endure a drag queen story hour? We must protect our children's innocence. We must let children live in sexual innocence until the time they need to be taught by their parents.

Moreover, will we allow AI (artificial intelligence) to teach our children as well or will we give them DI, **DIVINE INTELLIGENCE?** News Guard, a radical fact checking group, now monitors the Internet. They designate with red labels and green labels. Green means they like you and approve of your content, and red means they think you deliver hate speech. They censor free speech. CNN and The New York Times have received a green label from them. They have a list of do's and don't's to receive a green label. Censorship has gone rampant. Truth no longer is a left-wing value. We must fight for free speech. We defend our amendments of freedom of speech and freedom of religion. Why do they wish to silence us? Because faith comes by hearing and hearing by the Word of God! It's time the church stops being politically correct and becomes prophetically correct! The church of Jesus Christ started America, and we must continue to lead America!

No phrase has been more misunderstood and misapplied than Thomas Jefferson's wall of separation between church and state. It was a line he used in the Danberry Baptist conference in 1802. The statement fed the fires and extreme liberals in America who were trying to eradicate references to God and Christ in the public square. He made the statement to protect the church from the state not the state from the church.

We must refuse to hide and live in fear. We must refuse to be cowards. In fact, God says in Revelation 21:8 that He does not like cowards, and they will have their part in the lake of fire. That's tight, but it's right! But the good news is that God always has a plan. He always knows how to ambush the enemy, and He makes surprise attacks from a concealed position. The scripture says, "when the enemy comes in, like a flood the Lord raises up a standard," and "what the enemy has done for evil, God always turns for our good." The narrative of this day demands a healer, a reconciler, a deliverer, a savior, solution-makers, and change-agents, I pray it's you!

Jesus told His disciples "Go YE into all the world." Jesus was speaking of the world systems. Then He told them, "When you go bring your peace on them," meaning they come under your influence. Peace is a Presence, and peace is an influence and an authority. Peace is a state of infectious domination. It's an internal condition that you possess because you have Christ in you. May I say it this way? Soften your heart but harden your forehead.

The word culture derives from the word cultivate. When bringing in a new culture (the Kingdom), it's important to cultivate (develop, prepare, labor) the soil of that environmental landscape. To change the culture of a city, you will need unified intercessory prayer teams, prophetic proclamations, apostolic crisis teams, and a convergence and emerging together of fivefold leaders and entrepreneurs.

And he spake many things unto them in parables, saying, Behold, a sower went forth to sow; and when he sowed, some seeds fell by the way side, and the fowls came and devoured them up: some fell upon stony places, where they had not much earth: and forthwith they sprung up, because they had no deepness of earth: and when the sun was up, they were scorched; and because they had no root, they withered away. And some fell among thorns; and the thorns sprung up, and choked them: but other fell into good ground, and brought forth fruit, some an hundredfold, some sixtyfold, some thirtyfold. Who hath ears to hear, let him hear."- Matthew 13:3-9 KJV

This parable has multiple prophetic implications:

1) *Wayside*: represents religious environments that devour the seed. Religion is out of the Way, lost its way, fallen off the path, impenetrable (soil contaminated by religion). The wayside is in the following: Islam, Judaism, satanism, scientology, paganism, deism, and other unrighteous systems (including many denominations).

2) *Stony soil*: signifies hard, calloused, and bitter environments with no root. The stony soil can be seen in hopeless landscapes, economically disadvantaged soil, (soil hardened through deterioration and debilitation). It also includes educational systems that indoctrinate students with non-biblical philosophies and ungodly media platforms.

3) *Thorns*: denote cursed environments that choke the seed of a community. The thorns are found in negative words, wrong attitudes, generational curses caused by calamity, recession, evil leaders, secret societies, traumatic experiences, racist spirits, and soil cursed by wickedness.

Therefore, we must cultivate new soil by removing the stones, eliminating the thorns, and breaking up the fallow ground.

Seeding Your City

- The seed must come into covenant with the soil (it must marry the soil).
- There is nothing wrong with the seed, only the soil.
- The seed has 100% germination potential.
- You can't have a harvest without a seed; that's a Kingdom principle.
- Never call the land by its present appearance, but by the seed!
- Every seed sown has its own instruction; its DNA produces after its kind!
- Your words have divine instructions.
- Your faith is not in the soil but the seed!
- Take your eyes off the soil!
- Put your faith in the seed!
- The seed tells the soil what it needs.

Isaiah 55:11 states, "So shall the Word BE (become) that goes out of my mouth. It shall not return to me void but it shall accomplish that which I please and it shall prosper where I sent it!" God has so much faith in His seed which is His Word. He believes it will become what He says! WHY?

The Law of Sowing and Reaping

- We seed the future of our city; the city becomes the womb of the seed.
- When the seed originates in the Spirit then the Holy Ghost will overshadow it!
- With God nothing shall be impossible (with the seed nothing shall be impossible)!
- Mary said, "How shall these things be SEEING...." Quit seeing and start sowing!

- Prophecy and pray out the future of your city.
- SOW prayer seeds in barren structures (e.g. Ezekiel prophesied over dead bones).
- Breathe life into old structures. Sow Kingdom seeds in barren ground!
- Leaders are Seeders...we sow seeds of success into our cities.

Historically, there are tipping points in culture. One was in 1963 that leaned the pendulum away from the Kingdom of God. Let's look at some statistics. Since 1963, premarital sex increased 500%, sexually transmitted diseases went up 200%, suicides went up 400%, SAT scores dropped 90 points from 1963 to 1980 (which was the lowest in the world). Single parent families went up 140%, violent crime went up 500% and unwed pregnancy went up 400%.

The church baby boomers did a poor job as gatekeepers during their spiritual watch over this nation. But a new tipping point is here for the pendulum is swinging back in favor of the Kingdom of Heaven, and it's called "GLORY DOMINION." Our finest hour is upon us. It's time for the kings in God's Kingdom to arise, so they can rule and reign. To reign simply means to change things. Examine the history of your city to prepare for your city's transformation.

What is the History of Your City?

Prepare your city for the glory of God by studying the history of your city. Below is a list of questions you will need to answer:

1. What were the religious practices of early settlers?
2. What were the traits of past leadership?

3. Did our city have a founder and what was his dream?
4. What dominating forces have governed our city? Political, economic, religious?
5. What is the history among the races?
6. What traumatic experiences hit our city?
7. Who leads the city spiritually?

The Family Mountain: Blessing the Families of the Earth

Now the LORD had said unto Abram, Get thee out of thy country, and from thy kindred, and from thy father's house, unto a land that I will shew thee: and I will make of thee a great nation, and I will bless thee, and make thy name great; and thou shalt be a blessing: and I will bless them that bless thee, and curse him that curseth thee: and in thee shall all families of the earth be blessed. - Genesis 12:1-3 KJV

Every apostolic and prophetic network within the city must create a vision for blessing the families and their city. Some ideas include the following:
- Feeding the poor
- Evangelizing
- Building quality homes
- Developing after-school programs for children in the community
- Establishing Chambers of Commerce for raising up emerging Kingdom entrepreneurs
- Creating and implementing Exodus programs for people with addictions
- Creating new jobs
- And the list goes on and how we bless the families of our cities.

For example, during the 2020 pandemic, we quickly noticed a need within our community for food. Within a short time, we developed the "THE NOW PROJECT" (Nourishing Others' Well-being). As a result of this, we currently feed approximately 1,600 families every month. During the food giveaways, our intercessors minister and pray for them as they lineup for the distribution. This is one method of blessing the families that God has placed under your care.

For too long, the church has been speaking and entertaining the idea of a life hereafter in Heaven, without impacting our present world. The church has been preaching God's Word without demonstrating how it works. But now, we are moving into a season of demonstration. Long enough, the church has offered rhetorical encouragement for the plight of the poor without developing an economy to alleviate the plight of the poor. The Kingdom of God does not just talk about the answer; **it is the answer** and demonstrates the answer. DESTINY IS IN OUR HANDS as we reach the families in our cities.

It's Time to Take the Media Mountain!

One of the first mountains that the church must recover is the mountain of media. Malcolm X once said, "The media is the most powerful entity on earth. They have the power because they control the minds of the masses." Whoever has the most hope has the most influence! And influence is the capacity to affect the character, thoughts, and behavior of a person or group.

As Ezra the priest, in the book of Nehemiah, boldly spoke on behalf of heaven, we also must rise up, stand up and boldly proclaim heaven's message to influence and call forth the destiny of our cities, our states and even our nation. Thus, we will lead nations back to our heavenly Father.

Any believer, radically saved, filled with heaven's Holy Ghost, and transformed by the power of Jesus Christ, carries a weight of glory and the reality of hope within them. Paul said, "It is a hope that does not disappoint!" The world craves hope! Hell wants the world to feel hopeless, intent on stealing their dreams and their identity.

Our nation is waking up from a deep sleep and now they are desperate for truth. Yet, most Christians are sound asleep, lukewarm, and passionless. While the alarm has been sounding, they have been hitting the snooze button.

But there is a small remnant emerging with HOPE beating in their breasts. Emerging with courage and a voice of Truth, they embody a voice of hope and demonstrate the power of God to their generation. They walk in signs and wonders, displaying the goodness of God to humanity. They are a Kingdom-driven generation of men, women, boys, and girls who are intimately passionate with Jesus Christ. These saints of the Most High God are on fire and know how to bring God's glory and fire into their world, thus creating transformation.

Wealth Creation

Every city needs a Kingdom Chamber of Commerce with the purpose and intent to create wealth to establish the Kingdom of God in their city for His purposes.

But thou shalt remember the Lord thy God: for it is he that giveth thee power to get wealth, that he may establish his

covenant which he sware unto thy fathers, as it is this day. -
Deuteronomy 8:18

Wealth cannot be transferred under weak, anemic
governments. It is only released under the righteous
governments where citizens thrive! We see the pattern with
Moses and the children of Israel. Moses was an apostle and
a prophet in his time leading the Israelites. Under his
administration all twelve tribes prospered for 40 years
under the most horrific circumstances. In this new season,
God is not sparing resources for Kingdom advancement. A
new level of urgency is upon Kingdom citizens to rise,
prepare, and impact the infrastructure of our society with
the culture of Heaven and the Kingdom of our Christ.
Every Kingdom network needs a vision to raise up a new
breed of Kingdom entrepreneurs and wealth builders.
Trained, empowered, and equipped, they become economic
engines and custodians of wealth who revitalize landscapes,
reform communities, and heal economies within cities and
nations.

Jesus taught, "Blessed are the meek for they *shall inherit
the Earth*." He did not say blessed are the meek for they
shall inherit heaven. Therefore, He promised us real estate.
As the seed of Abraham, we've been promised land. The
word meek in the Hebrew language means: controlled
power and self-discipline.

*A good man leaveth an inheritance to his children's
children: And the wealth of the sinner is laid up for the just.*
- Proverbs 13:22 KJV

The world is facilitating wealth until we get ready to
manage it. We truly should be ashamed of this verse; it's an
indictment against us. God has given the world the money
because they are currently managing it better than us. God

gives money to managers. We can prophesy all we want about money, but now, with what we have, let's be good managers. Although Christians, have been declaring, "Money cometh, money cometh." Although naming and claiming wealth, they still don't have money.

Lazy hands make for poverty, but diligent hands bring wealth. - Proverbs 10:4 NIV

Lazy people want much but get little, but those who work hard will prosper. - Proverbs 13:4 NLT

The slothful man does not catch his game or roast it once he kills it, but the diligent man gets precious possessions. - Proverbs 12:27 AMPC

When a company fires an employee, it's usually because they're lazy. Remember this: money doesn't leave the planet. It only runs and hides. If you mismanage money, it will run from you.

No man can serve two masters: for either he will hate the one, and love the other; or else he will hold to the one, and despise the other. Ye cannot serve God and mammon. - Matthew 6:24(KJV)

The church of Jesus Christ must structure and build accurate systems and implement processes and protocols to help prepare and empower the saints for wealth creation and wealth transfer. It's time to build the Kingdom; therefore, it's time to build new systems to create wealth. Wealth management is a Kingdom mandate. It's time the church of Jesus Christ develops a strong and diverse portfolio of inventions, products, ideas, houses, lands, and resources. Through the process of buying and selling what we have, we will benefit the Kingdom community at large and advance the Apostolic-Prophetic visions for our city.

The Lord expects us to take dominion. The time has come that we make an impressive march towards the goals of birthing, developing, and supporting Kingdom businesses which are owned and operated by the saints. When such businesses are created with the spirit of excellence, quality, and integrity, God is glorified, and then, in return, He will favor and bless that business.

Increasing money without a Kingdom model only increases demonic activity. Wherever there is wealth, there will be demons in the shadows. Within the world there are several harlot systems that rule the mountain of finance:

- **Pharaoh's system** enslaves people to work harder and to keep people enslaved in poverty (Exodus 1:13,14).

- **The Pharisaical system** restricts people from entering their destinies. It's a system that doesn't want you to succeed (Matt. 23:13).

- **The Babylonian system** puts man in bondage. It is a harlot system that keeps you in debt and keeps you from occupying the mountain of finance (Rev. 7:9).

Remember the woman with the issue of blood? She had sought out many physicians as a remedy to her problem but none of them worked. She had to find a Kingdom model that was greater than the worldly systems. When she touched Jesus, her hemorrhaging stopped. For every demonic system there is a Kingdom model that outranks the worldly systems. Naming, claiming and rebuking devils over your money will change nothing! You need a new model, a new system, to increase your wealth, so you can penetrate the world's structures and recover their spoils.

And thou say in thine heart, My power and the might of mine hand hath gotten me this wealth. But thou shalt remember the LORD thy God: for it is he that giveth thee power to get wealth, that he may establish his covenant which he sware unto thy fathers, as it is this day. - Deuteronomy 8:17-18 (KJV)

Now the just shall live by faith: but if any man draw back, my soul shall have no pleasure in him. - Hebrews 10:38(KJV)

Finances follow faith; your faith doesn't follow your finances. You need a Kingdom cause, a vision, coupled with faith that is the foundation for wealth creation. Innate in every believer is the power to create wealth. Please notice: He doesn't give us wealth, but He gives us the power to create wealth. What is the power to create wealth? The power is found in vision, wisdom, character, skill, innovation, partnership, networking, excellence, stewardship, anointing, relationships, maturity, education, and the list goes on. You don't need money; you need power. Joseph had no money, but he had power, and he became God's wallet. As you can see, it is much more than money, but a host of power points.

And God said, Let us make man in our image, after our likeness: and let them have dominion over the fish of the sea, and over the fowl of the air, and over the cattle, and over all the earth, and over every creeping thing that creepeth upon the earth. So God created man in his own image, in the image of God created he him; male and female created he them.

And God blessed them, and God said unto them, Be fruitful, and multiply, and replenish the earth, and subdue it: and have dominion over the fish of the sea, and over the fowl of the air, and over every living thing that moveth upon the earth. - Genesis 1:26-28 KJV

You and I were created to demonstrate rulership, which means management over creation. We are all the master of something in the planet. The gift of stewardship and dominion is resident within you. Adam was given dominion and stewardship. God blessed Adam and Eve for their purpose. The blessing released ability. We are in season where the Lord has blessed and empowered us to release our abilities and God-given gift clusters. God created one man, only one, then He pro-created. God put Adam into one body, then took a woman out of his womb. The Lord blessed them, and said, "Be fruitful, multiply, replenish the earth, subdue it, and have dominion.

What has the Lord placed within you? What is your gift cluster? God has given you power to release it and become fruitful. You and I were created to be managers. Poor management will attract poverty, while good management always attract prosperity. Cities fall into recession and fail to prosper for one reason, and one reason alone: poor management. Management is the effective use of resources. We have been given a management mandate to exercise the giftings and abilities that God has given us so we can master and manage the Earth. Resources move to managers. Close to 10,000 churches have closed since the Covid pandemic. Because of the mismanagement of those churches, they've lost people and resources. If they would have maximized what they had, their doors would not be closed today. Indeed, it's a divine ordination and mandate for such a time as this for the saints to CREATE WEALTH and DETERMINE DESTINY!! Below, I've given areas in which I suggest that you invest in. Invest in 6 areas:

1) the church
2) silver/gold
3) medicine (homeopathic)
4) energy
5) technology
6) property/land

Natural resources are God's economy. To order your copy of Wealth Creation mp3 please go to: drmarkkauffman.org.

Kingdom Education: A Model University

The Lord has called us to the mountain of education. Below is the vision of Kingdom International University (KIU) to give you an example of Kingdom education.

Kingdom International University prepares men and women of all ages as local church leaders and those leaders called to marketplace ministry. Through the truths of apostolic doctrine and a Biblical world view, KIU seeks to transform society by preparing students for life and careers that will help to shape and directly engage the world and influence culture.

Christian higher education has strayed from equipping and empowering the church to raise up a new generation of change-agents. Through college level education we have lost influence in the marketplace and in the public square. We have lost our voice and must recover it. We must regain the platform of trading ideas in the marketplace. Ideas have consequences and ideas not influenced by truth have deadly results. Today the god of education is knowledge that is not based upon truth; moreover, it's knowledge without understanding and wisdom.

Our intent is not to operate as indoctrinators of Christianity, but to create a Kingdom template that promotes individuals to interact with God and impact society. Our foundation template is the seven spheres of society in which we teach our students to thrive at the head of culture.

We are using a new wealth of divine curricula that carry the virtue, purpose, and anointing of the Spirit of God. Most Christian curriculum is outdated and void of present-day truth. We are called to teach our generation to:

- *Discover who they are in Christ.*
- *Then determine what they have in Christ.*
- *Then develop what they have in Christ.*
- *Then display what they have in Christ.*

The Kingdom of God is Disruptive and Demonstrative

That which is in chaos and crisis is that which is built and empowered by the kingdom of darkness. The powers of darkness are working overtime to circumvent truth. A compliant media under their command has aided that attempt. The unleashing of massive misinformation has almost half the population momentarily under their demonic influence.

Thus saith the Lord; remove the diadem and takeoff the crown: this shall not be the same, exalt him that has low and abase him that is high. I will overturn, overturn, overturn, and it shall be no more until he come who's right it is and I will give it to him. - Ezekiel 21:26, 27

The NIV says, "Remove the diadem and takeoff the crown, the old order is changing."

The good news about everything in this moment is that we are in the throes of a Kingdom Overturn (to overpower, to conquer, to overthrow, to make to bow down). In Ezekiel 21:26,27, the NIV says, "A ruin, a ruin, a ruin, I will make it a ruin." We're now coming into a triple overthrowing of the powers of darkness. Philippians 2:10 declares, "That at the name of Jesus every knee should bow of things in heaven and things in earth, and things under the earth." There is now an overturning of the enemy's plans, and we shall overcome evil with good!

Jesus Christ is the legal covenantal owner of everything in Heaven and earth and under the earth. He is the heir to all things. We are heirs of God and joint heirs with Jesus. Liken this idea to when the spirit of Elijah fell upon Elisha.

The zeal of the Lord will fulfill the justice mandate as the cries and the blood of the abused children have put a demand on Him. He will not back off from their petitions. The cries of the children enslaved to sex trafficking put a demand on the Judge of All Ages to respond with justice. The coming exposures and judgments will shock the world and bring a reassessment of history that will make this time one of those "before and after" sequences when the lines are drawn in the sand, and it will be remembered forever. History makers are emerging to fulfill Kingdom conquest. Voices coming out of the wilderness will be heard in our land!

The World is in Chaos and the Kingdom of God is Thriving

This present crisis is the last battle you will have to go through before moving into your destiny. While you are going through the process, God is taking down the enemy. You are being ushered into your kingship like David and his final battle at Ziklag. Similarly, God is ushering you into your purpose. Something supernatural is in the process. Be confident that something huge is coming our way because of the chaos. We have been "average" for too long. Release average, release your past, release status quo for there is something greater in front of you. Under this canopy of darkness, a miracle is in process. It's a "without-fail" season!

If you follow the world news we seem to be in a major revolutionary time of great upheaval and social unrest. Criminals and/or illegitimate governments are stealing or attempting to steal elections in nation after nation. Uprisings demanding more freedom and counter uprisings funded by socialists/globalists are popping up all over the globe. Count these as just some of the nations that are experiencing winds of this kind of revolution: the United States, Canada, France, the Netherlands, Lebanon, Chile, Ecuador, Peru, Israel, Hong Kong/China, Bolivia, Honduras, Nicaragua, and the UK. Amid this alarming chaos where seemingly everything is at risk, I have one clear announcement to you: THE KINGDOM OF GOD IS THRIVING! God is on the move and a massive global, extreme makeover is upon us. The kingdom of darkness is in the first stage of being decimated (ruled over), and yes, the Kingdom of God is disruptive to it.

Hebrews 12:25-29 describes this truth and a scenario that is being played out now on planet Earth. While not the final fulfillment of it, what we are seeing is a present fulfillment of this passage. It is a time when God's voice comes and shakes everything that can be shaken. We have entered a decade of His voice shaking all. As He exposes what should be shaken, He dislodges it and positions us for verse 28 which says, "we are receiving an unshakable Kingdom." But this requires the kings to arise and to be voices of reconciliation, restoration, restitution, and reformation in our cities!

Appendix: Resources for Your City

- Can you do it?
- Will you do it?
- How will you do it?
- With whom will you do it?
- When will you do it?

CHRISTIAN CHAMBER OF COMMERCE OF PENNSYLVANIA: EMPOWERING PEOPLE TO EMPOWER VISION

Below is the vision and mission statement for the Christian Chamber of Commerce of Pennsylvania. At the chamber it is our purpose and intent to serve other communities by empowering Kingdom business men and women and aspiring entrepreneurs. If you would like a branch of the chamber in your city and region, we would be honored to help you establish a chamber for the purpose of advancing the Kingdom of God through businesses in your region.

> There are many people with great vision, but great vision that is not empowered, is no vision at all; it remains a dream, and never becomes a reality. The purpose and intent of the Christian Chamber of Commerce of Pennsylvania (CCCP) is to be committed to your success. If you're maintaining instead of growing, CCCP is for you! Our empowerment tracks will equip you to succeed and not just survive. Our mission philosophy, along with our empowerment tracks, vast leadership acumen, and innovative programming empower our members to create wealth, impact the community,

and fulfill their divine destinies. Join us, become a member at CCCP and watch your visions transition from your dreams into reality.

Today's battlefield is for kings in the marketplace. We are called to help men and women catch the revelation that they are going to war Monday through Friday to do great exploits. To be providers for the Kingdom of God births real life focus! When the Kingdom is only a weekend event, man's need and passion for conquest is misplaced. When kings do not have a clear vision as providers of the Kingdom, their need for conquest will be misdirected. King David was called to be on the battlefield, but stayed home and was found in the bedroom with Bathsheba. This is called misplaced conquest, leading men to other sinful or nonproductive fulfillments and activities! This type of conquest leads to self-indulgence, self-pity, and other sins! Man was created for conquest and adventure, and doing business supernaturally in the marketplace fulfills conquest and adventure.

The Christian Chamber of Commerce of Pennsylvania is committed to the establishment of synergistic partnerships between business, church, and government entities for the greater purpose of reintegrating communities with biblical values, and restoring the traditional family, espousing the love of God, love of family and the love of country.

We further commit ourselves to the challenge of restoring new hope within our cities. CCCP is raising up a new breed of leaders that are endowed with excellent work ethic, thereby eliminating the ravaging generational curses of welfare and poverty within cities and states. Through the development of community-based educational and biblical programs, we are committed to mentoring and crafting individuals as morally responsible citizens, who are holistic in body, mind, and spirit.

The chamber is committed to the economic revitalization of our communities, therefore, fostering a greater society within their cities and states. We are committed to restoring the pride of authorship, whereby businesses are owned, and operated by members of their community and not absentee business owners. This is the spirit of community entrepreneurs in which, love for the community enables them to serve with excellence, honor, and generosity.

BUSINESS TRACK MODULES

- Creating economic synergy
- Doing business supernaturally
- The spirit of the community entrepreneur
- Focused vision
- The power of succession
- Raising up risk engenders
- Power to create wealth
- Defying the status quo
- Honor in the marketplace
- Business excellence
- The power of increase
- Fellowship builds relationship
- Surviving or succeeding
- Building a Kingdom business
- Create disciples not employees
- The power of partnership

- Business incubation
- Training for reigning
- The spirit of generosity
- Designing destiny
- Servanthood leadership
- The power of influence
- Marketplace ministers
- The church in the marketplace

www.ingramcontent.com/pod-product-compliance
Lightning Source LLC
Chambersburg PA
CBHW052044270326
41931CB00012B/2621

* 9 7 9 8 9 8 9 2 6 0 2 2 5 *